KING CITY

In loving memory of Paddy Dalton ...
Rest easy, my friend.

Paddy Dalton and his partner, Kelly.

Paddy, Aairon, and Eli.

KING CITY

ADVENTURES INTO BIRMINGHAM'S DIVERSE MUSIC CULTURE

STEPHEN PENNELL

ALSO BY THE AUTHOR:

STAR-SPANGLED VILLANS

GANGSTERS, GEEZERS AND MODS

First published 2021

The History Press
97 St George's Place,
Cheltenham,
Gloucestershire,
GL50 3QB
www.thehistorypress.co.uk

British Library Cataloguing in Publication Data.
A catalogue record for this book is available from the British Library.

ISBN 978 0 7509 9628 0

Typesetting and origination by Typo•glyphix, Burton-on-Trent
Printed and bound by TJ Books Limited, Padstow, Cornwall

CONTENTS

DEDICATION TO PADDY DALTON

A As final preparations were being made for the publication of this book, I received a phone call from a friend, Bod Phillips, with the heartbreaking news that I – we – had lost our friend Paddy Dalton in tragic circumstances. The call hit me hard. First, we lost Garry Twist and Paul 'Dinky' Drinkwater – two full-of-fun, larger-than-life characters (more of whom later) – and now Paddy.

My debut novel, Gangsters, Geezers and Mods, had just been published and was doing well, and just a week earlier I had told my wife Kerri of my plan to get Paddy involved in a follow-up. (Paddy's partner, Kelly, later told me that he would have loved to have written a book.) I had the story mapped out in my mind and wanted my mate to 'pad it out' (pun intended) with the kind of colour, experience, detail and humour that only he could bring. I wanted to go out for a drink with him and discuss it all, just the two of us. Whenever I saw Paddy, we were in a crowd and he'd be holding court, telling an enthralled audience his notoriously tall tales, everyone rolling around with laughter. Were they all true? Maybe not, but Paddy lived such an incredible life, you never knew for sure. Either way, I'll always be grateful that whatever company he was in, he always greeted me as a friend and never outed me as a Villa fan!

After the initial shock and grief, my mind dwelled on happier memories of a man who was the life and soul of every night out I was privileged to share with him. Due to Covid restrictions, I wasn't able to attend the funeral, so instead, I decided to pay my respects with this book and donate half my royalties from its sale to Kelly, the son he was so proud of, Aairon, and their family.

Of course, if you bought this book, that money comes from you, whether you were lucky enough to know him or not, so heartfelt thanks for your generosity. I'm just the treasurer. Paddy contributed more to good nights out in Brum than anyone (bar Eddie Fewtrell), so this book seems an appropriate place to pay tribute, and I've shared an amusing little story about him within its pages. I hope it makes you smile.

ACKNOWLEDGEMENTS

Thanks to those who were instrumental in the writing of this collection, especially my wife, soulmate and digital guru, Kerri Pennell; my mate and picture editor extraordinaire, Simon Pitt; my long-time editor, employer, mentor and friend, Dave Woodhall; Richard Franks, editor at Counteract; and Nicola Guy from The History Press, who worked so hard to get this book commissioned and was always ready with a calming message when I was panicked about something or other.

Inspiration was provided by everybody who features, too many to mention here, but especially AffieJam and Ben Ramsay (The New Consistent), who I am privileged to call my friends.

A big shout out to the brilliant photographers featured: Luke Jones, Paul Moreau, Phil Drury, Stewart Lawley, Soul Diggs, Dan Clayton, Taylor Wright, Rob Blackham, Lee Crawford and Matt Crockford.

Thanks to everyone who accompanied me on these adventures: my babies, Amber and Lewis Pennell; my grown-up kids, Kirsty, Kurtis and Tyler Cassin; my partner-in-crime, Mark Eagles; my mother-in-law Carmen Henry and auntie Angie Jackson; the indefatigable Jo Jeffries; Paul and Sam Schofield; Jordan Dillon, Russ James, Jason Rhodes, Gay Morse, Mark Carter, Lee Byrnes, Jason Donnelly, Peter Rogers, Paul and Louis Caffrey, Courtney Hearne, Russell and Jo Collier, Mark and David Jackson, Lizzie Halpin, Tony Baldwin, Paddy Ryan, Gary Williams, Steve O'Connor, Steve Turner, Steve Sainy, Jerome Falconer, Carlos Malcolm, Filthy Phil and Long-Haired Lou.

Thanks also to Phil and Jim McLaughlin, Kelly Wagstaff, Aairon Dalton, Carl Chinn, Richard Whitehead, Sam Lambeth, Lee Williams, Mark Moore, Stuart Palmer, Chris Waldron, Dave Scrivens, Darren Kierney, Lynn Ryan, Sharon Walker, Joanne Carberry, Michael Taylor, Chris Bushell, Paul Collins (the Gabbie Cabbie), Gavin Monaghan, Roger Davis, Adrian Goldberg, Mazzy Snape, Robert and Amanda Hill, Sara Coleman, Robert Hayden, Lisa Smith and Chris Sutton for their friendship and support.

INTRODUCTION

Birmingham is probably the most creative city on earth – of 4,000 patents registered in the UK each year, 2,800 come from Brum – but the perception of it rarely lives up to the reality. Half the people who live here haven't got a good word to say about the place, and from further afield the brickbats are even worse. The BBC have abandoned us, run off with our TV licence money, turned Pebble Mill into a dental hospital and shacked up with Manchester. We've had a lot of good press in the print media lately, but they always seem to preface even the most positive article with, 'We know it's terrible but it's not as bad as you think'. Yet, the negativity towards the birthplace of the modern world seems to be a peculiarly British phenomenon, and I sometimes feel like telling the rest of the country that if we'd known you were going to be like this, we wouldn't have bothered building all those Spitfires.

But don't be disheartened fellow Brummies – there's a big world out there and lots of it loves us. A while ago, a portion of England seemed in danger of losing its marbles over the Stone Roses reunion, mainly due to the fact they're from Blow-Your-Own-Trumpetsville. Elsewhere, a comeback by Black Sabbath, a much bigger and more influential band, went comparatively unheralded. In the end, the Roses played a couple of big gigs in parks slightly smaller than Sutton's before their comeback fizzled out to nothing, while Sabbath set off on a massive world tour and released an album, 13, that went to number one in the States, Canada, the UK and numerous other countries.

The Sabbath story is probably the Brummiest ever told. Tony Iommi was on his last shift at the sheet metal works before committing full time to music when disaster struck as he accidentally chopped off the ends of two fingers. Instead of giving up, like a cockney would, he made thimbles to protect his damaged digits and when he played guitar with them, discovered he'd invented heavy metal. Resourceful and revolutionary – just like his hometown. More recently, I was on holiday in Mexico and many I spoke to had a refreshingly high opinion of Birmingham culture, be it J. R. R. Tolkien, Lee Child or Peaky Blinders. I met fans of UB40, ELO and Duran Duran, and everybody just LOVED Ozzy. I mentioned

Oasis, Joy Division and the Roses, which proved to be useful research – if you were researching the various ways different nationalities do blank looks.

It's hard to say when my obsession with Greater Birmingham music began. It could have been when the Guardian heralded Peace as the future of indie, the NME hailed The Twang as 'the best new band in Britain', or when I saw Lady Leshurr performing 'No Scrubs' with my daughter at a school concert. Perhaps it goes back to my teenage years in Marston Green hanging around with Miles Hunt, who went on to front the Wonder Stuff, or even further to when my little mate in Chelmsley Wood had a nan from Aston who knew Black Sabbath and a big brother who had signed copies of all their LPs.

Bear with me as I examine our rich musical heritage more closely. A good place to start is with The Wonder Stuff who, along with Pop Will Eat Itself and Ned's Atomic Dustbin, were the leading lights of a Stourbridge-born music phenomenon that raised its unkempt head back in the eighties. The bands were all pals and shared certain musical and sartorial similarities, so the music press had to come up with a name for it: 'grebo'. The term claimed the cultural zeitgeist for a while, most notably when The Stuffies teamed up with Reeves and Mortimer for their number one hit 'Dizzy'.

I didn't see them in the course of writing this book, but I mention them here because they encompass the second city's modus operandi – producing understated, unheralded brilliance with very little hype and fanfare, in much the same way as the Moody Blues invented prog rock, Sabbath invented heavy metal, and a few kids including Napalm Death messed about at the Mermaid in Sparkhill and created grindcore.

The NME rightly credits the city as being 'one of the few places not situated by the Mississippi River that can legitimately claim to have birthed a musical genre'. Close, but no cigar. Try FIVE genres – heavy metal, prog rock, bhangra, grebo and grindcore – and massive influence on and contributions to lots of others.

Any potted summary of Midlands musical innovation must also mention Duran Duran and Dexy's Midnight Runners, while Sabbath's ex-manager Jim Simpson's assertion that Birmingham is the rock capital of the world stands up to scrutiny when one remembers his former charges plus Stevie Winwood, The Move, ELO, Judas Priest and Led Zeppelin, and the fact that a young woman from Bearwood (Christine McVie) wrote some of the best songs on Fleetwood Mac's Rumours – one of the biggest-selling albums of all time.

And that's just the white people. Joan Armatrading was the first black British female musician to achieve international success, closely followed by another Brummie – Jaki Graham – and the roll-call from that particular demographic is nothing short of phenomenal. Add Jamelia, Ruby Turner and Beverley Knight to the list and note that three of the last five best female winners at the MOBOS – Laura Mvula, Lady Leshurr and Stefflon Don – were born in Brum. Coming soon: Jorja Smith and Mahalia.

Birmingham was also the birthplace (and subsequently the international HQ) of bhangra, and who can forget the domination of reggae record sales by UB40, Steel Pulse and Musical Youth, whose promo for 'Pass the Dutchie' was the first black video ever played on MTV?

Back in the now, Mike Skinner's documentary The Unstoppable Rise of Birmingham Rap explores the vibrant urban scene, while The Streets, Call Me Unique, Mahalia and Jorja Smith all impressed at the last Glastonbury Festival.

Lady Sanity and Namywa are not just super-talented, but also absolute soldiers for the city, and Lotto Boyzz, Mist, Dapz On The Map, Stardom, Mitch, M1l-lionz and Jaykae are doing bits worldwide, the latter having had a song played on glamorous US TV series Power, and bestowed credibility on a remix of Ed Sheeran's chart topper, 'Take Me Back To ...' – nah, I ain't typing that!

It's no surprise that the BBC recently filmed two series of The Rap Game UK in the first city of UK rap. Meanwhile, hoping to reclaim our rightful place in the rock and pop mainstream, The Clause and The Novus are the nuclear option, Cage Park, Sugarthief and Spilt Milk Society provide the indie songcraft, while B-Town pioneers The Twang, Peace, Swim Deep and JAWS have shown admirable staying power with fourteen albums between them.

So, why does this huge, impactful success and talent go seemingly unnoticed, not by the rest of the world, just the rest of the country? Our incredible diversity is undoubtedly a good thing, but in terms of marketing, does it work against us? Jimmy Brown of UB40 thinks it might:

Most other cities have a sort of identity. The Liverpool sound, the Manchester sound, even London has a musical identity. But Birmingham is so diverse it encompasses many different styles. How do you find a link between bands like Black Sabbath, Duran Duran and UB40, and everything in between?

It could be a geographical thing, he reasons:

We are just about the only UK city that hasn't grown out of a port. Ports have a different culture, they're more transient, and there are strong links to the homelands of any incomers. With Birmingham, people are plonked down in the middle of the country and just told to get on with it. So we did. I was born and raised in Small Heath and that was a privilege. You could sit on your doorstep and watch the four corners of the world pass by.

Birmingham's tradition of individualism and experimentation, and the unusually fragmented but innovative culture that results, has been widely remarked upon by commentators. New York-based urbanist Jane Jacobs described Birmingham as one of the world's great examples of urban creativity, 'a great, confused laboratory of ideas ... a muddle of oddments that grew through constant diversification'. The historian G.M. Young contrasted the 'experimental, adventurous, diverse' culture of Birmingham with the 'uniform' culture of Manchester. And that applies to the city's contemporary music scene, just as it does to our cultural and industrial heritage, which goes some way to explaining why the Birmingham sound is hard to define and package. Also, English music journalists and taste-makers tend to be middle-class ex-students, so it is natural for them to praise the music of middle-class ex-students. But most of Birmingham's musicians have been defiantly working class, which is perhaps why our music strikes more of a chord with blue-collar international audiences, and why Manchester's doesn't.

Another problem is our natural humility. Miles Hunt, frontman of the aforementioned Wonder Stuff, explains:

> *Every band we met from Liverpool and Manchester would tell us they were the best band in the world. You would never hear Noddy Holder of Slade say that because he didn't need to. That's because people from the Midlands are generally comfortable in their own skin, which not only enables them to have wonderfully self-deprecating senses of humour, but also removes any need for them to brag about themselves. It is part of their enduring charm.*

But in this new decade, things are changing. We're never going to be a city of swaggering egos, with heads too big to fit through the doors at Digbeth Dining Club, but there are signs that we are learning how to shine a light on our city. Credit for this goes not only to the plethora of exciting indie bands, sick rappers and emotive singer-songwriters, but also to the collective of DJs, producers, pro- moters, venues, photographers, bloggers and vloggers that surrounds and promotes them.

There's an agglomeration building and coalescing around the Birmingham Music Awards, run by Jo Jeffries, whose unashamed mission is to relay and amplify this 0121 uprising to the world. And it's working. As The Zine UK pointed out in an article published in 2019, 'When The Brits TV show was yawning on in February, our Twitter was lit with chat about the Birmingham Music Awards'.

Birmingham Press and Richard Franks at Counteract are trying to get the message out by posting high-quality content all over the Internet and there were gigs by local artists almost every night of the week at the Hare and Hounds, the Sunflower Lounge, the Night Owl and a variety of other venues down Lower Trinity Street, before Covid. Call Me Unique's 'The Unique Experience' (every second Saturday of the month at Mama Roux's) was quite possibly the best night out in town – any town, open mic nights like 'Dope Vibes' and 'Neighbourhood', and networking events like the BMA monthly gatherings showcased the boundless energy and creativity of local artists, while Raw Sound TV gave them the chance to play up to the camera.

Studios like Vada, Bay 10, Pirate and Gavin Monaghan's legendary Magic Garden provide artists with priceless expertise and facilities. Home of Metal, curators of the recent Black Sabbath exhibition at the Birmingham Museum and Art Gallery, and Jez Collins with his much-anticipated Birmingham Music Museum, look after the heritage, while the future is in the capable hands of promoters like Mazzy Snape, Adam Reagan, Sonic Gun, This is Tmrw and the indefatigable Tim Senna, bigging up local music through his various radio gigs and documenting the indie scene via his riotous vlogs. Muna Ruumi (often the only hijab in the room) could talk for England, but chooses instead to speak up for Birmingham. On the radio are Alex Noble, who has a two-hour platform on BBC WM, which he uses to promote (tagline alert!) 'the best in unsigned, undiscovered and under-the-radar talent from the great West Midlands', plus Pete Steel and the crew at Brum Radio, which streams local music 24/7 from the Warehouse Café in Digbeth and provides a showcase for the very best of it with their A-list show. Adrian Goldberg's Adventures In Music is another two hours of essential listening for those who want to keep their ears to the ground and their fingers on the throbbing pulse of the vibrant local scene and beyond. For a reviewer like me, that's five or six hours a week of unmissable radio, and the most pleasurable day's work you could ever imagine.

Musical academia is well served by Lyle Bignon at Birmingham City University, Vix Perks at ACM, Jonny Amos at BIMM, Birmingham Ormiston Academy, South and City College and the Royal Birmingham Conservatoire, all churning out dozens of talented students. But what happens when they graduate? Venues are under attack from developers, who promote city living but make living in the city less attractive by displacing its culture. The Flapper has been saved from the wrecking ball but Scruffy Murphy's is under threat, so while the mantra of 'education, education, education' is a wise one, we need to support musicians' workplaces too.

I always wanted to be in a band – I'm proud of my city's huge contribution to musical history and would love to have added my own paragraph. I hated getting out of bed in the morning and becoming a rock-and-roll star seemed like the easy way out. But when I tried it I was terrible, and that was the end of that. So now, in a poacher-turned-gamekeeper scenario, this failed musician is honing his pen game, hoping to bask in the reflected glory of artists with actual talent, by writing reviews of Birmingham's finest up-and-coming performers, playing the city's most iconic venues for my website King City Online.

This book is a collection of the best and most significant features, the criteria for inclusion being that there have to be plenty of Birmingham references. I've included a few reviews of more established artists from here and elsewhere to hold the interest of the reader, although many people have been kind enough to say they enjoy them whether they've heard of the subject or not. I've tried to capture not only the performances, but some of the city's remarkable story, the genuine warmth between the stars and their audience, and most of all, the life that happens around the events. If you're unfamiliar with some of these artists, read on anyway. You will still be joining me on a cracking night out in Brum.

The book is part autobiography (all art is self-portrait), part travelogue, but every piece relates in some way to the place I call home. You will also find the odd interview with some of my favourite artists and influential figures in the city's creative sector. It meanders like Spaghetti Junction – largely dispensing with chronology – and I hope you enjoy the twists and turns.

The Birmingham music scene is about undeniable talent, irresistible beats and unpretentious fun. It's often said we lack glamour, but with Lady Leshurr and Jack Grealish repping us to the world, Tommy Shelby on telly and Steven Knight's plans to build TV and film studios in downtown Digbeth, that issue is being addressed. Soon, the only things we lack will be airs and graces, and you don't miss what you never had.

SP, 2021

MY BIRMINGHAM AND THE RAP GAME UK

I'm in Digbeth and all human life is here. During the day, creatives create in the Custard Factory, mods and hipsters hunt down vintage clothes, and blokes in grimy overalls build motorbikes or harvest salvageable bits from broken cars. The area is awash with social enterprises, beautiful churches, interesting architecture and an incredibly diverse population. Well-heeled hipsters rub shoulders with hard-up homeless, and barefoot babbies with wild hair play in the courtyard of the ramshackle flats above the coach station.

Later on, things will liven up even more as foodies arrive at Digbeth Dining Club, and *Peaky Blinders* tourists from all over the world follow Professor Carl Chinn on his walking tour somewhere over by the Rainbow and down Lower Trinity Street. Their paths will cross with locals meeting their mates for a big gig at the Institute, a little gig at Mama Roux's, or a sixties soul happening at the Night Owl. As dusk closes in, the paint on state-of-the-art graffiti murals and ancient ghost signs will appear to be the only thing stopping the higgledy-pig-gledy buildings from toppling over onto the streets they overlook, and queues of revellers will snake along the narrow pavements outside clubs that look like drop forges, mainly because they're converted drop forges.

This is the setting for the filming of a new BBC TV show, *The Rap Game UK*, in which seven promising MCs vie for a contract with Krept and Konan's record label, Play Dirty. The contestants have been put up in a swish apartment on the twenty-fifth floor of the Orion building, overlooking the Mailbox, but for this week's task they swap Yuppie paradise for the bear pit of the battle rap arena. The local underground MC community has been asked to stage a battle rap event – a clash – at which the TV hopefuls will cut their teeth on this most demanding of rap disciplines. Ghetts is there as a guest judge and Bison Briggs from Premier Battles is the host, charged with the responsibility of keeping some sort of order.

I'm here with the first family of battle rap – brothers Penance and Tydal (currently on an eight-clash-winning streak), and their sister Loxy, all-time champion of the long-running battle rap channel, King of the Ronalds. We make the most of the BBC catering – a Brummie has to get his money's worth out of the licence fee somehow, seeing as how most of it ends up in London and Manchester – and head back into the main room for the curtain raiser, a clash between Tydal from Brum and Termz, who's come up from The Smoke especially.

It's a mismatch. Termz is a little bit overweight and Tydal starts with the body shots:

> *It must have been hard in school for a fat kid,*
> *You couldn't do the things that the rest of the class did.*
> *For us it was 'heads, shoulders, knees and toes',*
> *For you it was 'heads, …*
> *Miss, I can't do the last bit'.*

Termz tried to come back, but his punches weren't landing, and he was on the ropes. Tydal moved in for the kill:

> *F*** Termz, I ain't gonna show him respect,*
> *I'd chin him, but look at this prick in the flesh.*
> *I'm not exactly sure which chin I should check,*
> *With his gross man-boobs and invisible neck,*
> *I'll punch him in the stomach for the ripple effect.*

The hometown crowd roared their approval and waited for the knockout. They didn't have to wait long:

> *'You f***** up Bro, this is my home,*
> *0121, welcome to my zone,*
> *It's gonna be tragic when your bros don't back it*
> *Realise in my postcode, ev'ryone savage.*
> *Thought you could come here and war with a god?*
> *I got this s*** in the bag like I'm walking the dog.*

You don't get knocked out in a battle rap (well, maybe sometimes), but the Brummie definitely won on a unanimous decision. You could sense the relief of the TV contestants that they would be battling against each other, and not against the seasoned pros. A bit like a crew of white-collar boxers walking into Cus D'amato's gym and finding out they're fighting that little balding bloke from Accounts, not a fresh-outta-jail Mike Tyson.

They did okay, I suppose. Freedom of Speech and Kico were pretty good, and Smooth won her battle courtesy of her opponent choking. Then a massive argument over Lady Ice's beloved, deceased aunt and a bizarre love triangle involving J Lucia and Krept or Konan's ex-girl kept things entertaining, even if the bars weren't up to much. The edit made the row look like it soon blew over, but in real time it went on for about half an hour. Krept and Konan were fuming and the floor manager and other members of the film crew had their heads in their hands – time is money for them, I suppose.

When the filming finished, we went outside and blinked furiously at the surprise daylight – we'd been in a club for three hours and had totally forgotten it wasn't even lunchtime yet. Our motley crew of MCs headed for Subside, a twenty-four-hour rock club with a punchbag machine and a pool table. One of the bar staff is a member of the Sealed Knot Society and had some of his props behind the bar, and it wasn't long until some of Birmingham's finest (and drunkest) grime clashers were running round the pool table wearing chain-mail helmets and wielding ferocious-looking broadswords. I wasn't sure if they were re-enacting the last English Civil War or practising for the almost inevitable next one.

As for the show, I'm not sure it conveys quite how difficult it is to stand out as a rapper when there are so many really good ones about. As Lady Leshurr once put it, 'A new MC is born every day of the week.' Still, it's an entertaining show, and mainstream exposure for the genre is welcome. It could have easily gone 'X-Factor Goes Grime', but it steers just to the right side of that and at least takes a much-maligned art form seriously enough to show the haters that it's not as easy as they might think.

But they dropped a clanger by editing out the real star, Tydal. It would have made for great TV had the camera crew followed him and his siblings, Loxy and Penance, around the city for rest of the day.

REMEMBER HOW WE STARTED

After writing about the fate and fortunes of Aston Villa for a variety of magazines, culminating in my first book *Star-Spangled Villans*, my passion for writing about music was ignited when a friend gave me tickets to see my idol, Paul Weller. He asked me to write a review in lieu of payment, and I came up with something like this for *Heroes and Villains* …

MY NEVER CHANGING MOOD – PAUL WELLER @ WOLVES CIVIC

Ever since this date was announced I'd been looking forward to my trip to the Wolverhampton Civic with the enthusiasm of a teenager going to his first gig. Weller shows always bring that out in me, despite having seen him what must be close to 100 times. I suppose it's the future-facing focus of The Man Himself that keeps things so fresh – he's ripped up more successful formulas than any other musician I can think of. He's in his fourth or fifth purple patch and it's one that shows no sign of abating anytime soon.

I was slow off the mark for tickets and they sold out in four hours, so I'd have been dealing with touts were it not for my mate, or more accurately his missus, who booked a holiday for this, of all weeks, bless her, and he ended up giving me his tickets. So thanks Chris, I hope you enjoy reading about what you missed.

The day started well for me before I'd even left Chelmsley. There was a bloke outside the White Hart with a winning betting slip worth £280. Sadly for him the bookies was shut and he was so desperate for the money he was willing to sell it for £130. I wasn't carrying that kind of cash but my mate Paul 'Dinky' Drinkwater was in the back bar and he was always carrying that kind of money. Dinky was a Brummie Arthur Daley, the unofficial Lord Mayor of our ends, with a big wedge of notes in his pocket and a big heart of gold in his chest – if he liked you. Now Dinky liked me, but there were a few he didn't, and this bloke was one of them.

'I wouldn't give him the steam off my proverbial,' he said, 'but if you can make money out of the div, I'll weigh in. Here's a hundred, offer him that. Give it me back tomorrow after the bookie opens.' The bloke took it and I had made one hundred and eighty almost as quickly and easily as a champion darts player – what a start to the night!

After a lifetime following him around the country, me and my mates Paddy, Filthy Phil and Long-Haired Lou were pretty confident that Weller would start weaving his magic at about a quarter to nine, so when we entered the venue at half eight-ish and saw him on stage, we went into a bit of a panic. We were re-lieved to find we'd only missed one song, albeit the magnificent title track to his 2010 album *Wake Up the Nation*, so first up for us was 'Sunflower'. So delighted were we that he has started playing this live again after a few years' absence, the four of us decided to head for the mosh pit. 'I don't care how long this lasts/we have no future/we have no past', I thought, and Weller sang.

The Surrey super-mod was in fine form, his voice as strong as ever despite the ravages of forty years of smoking and singing for a living, and I was thrilled by a fresh-sounding set list that could never be described as 'cabaret'. 'Sea-Spray' is one of my live faves, as is the electrifying 'Come On/Let's Go', played with the extra passion Paul always displays on his newer stuff. 'He's the Keeper', a touching tribute to late, great, Small Face Ronnie Lane, who died of MS, brought a lump to my throat and a tear to my eye, forcing me to stand in front of my mates so they couldn't see I was a bit choked up. ('He's the one knight/On a knackered stallion/His rusty armour/So undervalued/Doesn't know that/He's the reason/He's asleep now/But never gone').

Next up was 'Above the Clouds', a single from twenty years ago ('when I was 15,' said Weller), which was obviously written in one of his ridiculous phases of self-doubt – 'I have to wonder/Will I last?' As the enthralled crowd sang every word, I thought it safe to conclude he probably will!

I said on the way in that I hoped he wouldn't sing 'Porcelain Gods' as he sometimes drags out the guitar solo, but the power of the band and the bile and passion with which Weller spat the lyrics made it enjoyable again, despite his barbs at critics and reviewers – 'more empty words from the living dead/who seek to explain what can't really be said'. I tried not to blush.

A storming version of Weller's biggest Stateside hit 'My Ever-Changing Moods' was his solitary nod to the glorious Style Council era, which was a shame, as for a couple of years in the mid-eighties they were, in the opinion of me and the *Melody Maker*, 'probably the best pop group in the world'. 'The Attic', 'That Danger-ous Age', 'Going Places', 'Dragonfly' (co-written with his 10-year-old daughter), 'Picking up Sticks' and 'Be Happy Children' were all performed heroically and have great personal meaning to me, so it was getting pretty emotional again.

'Friday Street' was reinvigorated by a stunning new intro from Moseleyite guitar legend, Steve Craddock, then 'Start', 'Peacock Suit' and '7&3' made it pogo-time again. For the first encore, all the band came back on wearing garishly coloured capes – 'Don't ask,' said Weller – and threw a huge bouncing ball into the crowd. A reference to the iconic sixties TV show *The Prisoner* perhaps?

Anyway, it was all anthems from there on in – 'The Changingman', 'Out of the Sinking', 'Whirlpool's End', another break, another encore, 'A Town Called Malice' to finish. Great song though it undoubtedly is, I'm a bit sick of 'Malice' always closing his shows, but you can see why he plays it. It causes absolute mayhem in the mosh pit and contains two of the best couplets ever written: 'A whole streets belief/ in Sunday's roast beef/gets dashed against the Co-op/To either cut down on beer/ Or the kids' new gear/It's a big decision in a town called Malice!' all roared out by the crowd. Who is Weller to deny them their moment of terrible beauty?

What strikes me as impressive whenever I see him is what he doesn't play, a bit like judging the strength of a team by looking at the substitutes' bench. Career-defining anthems and classics like 'That's Entertainment', 'Wildwood', 'Tube Station', 'Eton Rifles', 'Going Underground', 'Into Tomorrow' – not played; truly great albums like *All Mod Cons, Setting Sons, Our Favourite Shop*, ignored; beautiful love songs like 'Long Hot Summer', 'English Rose', 'You're the Best Thing', 'You do Something to Me', kept under wraps. And yet the quality of the first team is such that you come out so sated you don't even notice what he didn't play until you're thinking about writing a review.

If I told you I went to a gig at which an artist missed out literally dozens of hits, anthems and showstoppers, you might be forgiven for thinking I left disappointed. But as that artist has a back catalogue including forty-year-old obscure B-sides that can put most songwriters to shame, you couldn't be more wrong. The bloke's a song-writing genius, a deadly live act, and a true modernist, always moving forward.

The evening ended in the pub round the corner, where my mate ordering a pint of Thatcher's Gold led to a lively few minutes slagging the grocer's daughter with all the hatred inspired by Weller (and some other stuff) all those years ago. It was as if we'd just walked out of a Style Council gig during the miners' strike.

So there you go, Chris, that's my review. Though of course, as clearly stated on *The Modern World* forty years ago – the subject of it don't give a damn about them.

STARR-STRUCK

D ave Woodhall, editor of *Heroes and Villains*, must have been impressed. He sent me press tickets to the VIP opening of the UK's only bespoke Northern Soul club, the Night Owl, in the hope that I'd write about it for his side hustle, the *Birmingham Press*. Unfortunately, I made a pig of myself on the complimentary champagne, and when I woke up the next afternoon, I couldn't remember a fat lot about it. But when I saw that Edwin Starr's brother, Angelo, was coming to town, I asked Dave to get me guest list again and promised to make a better fist of it this time …

ANGELO STARR AND THE TEAM @ THE NIGHT OWL

I'd seen Edwin Starr performing at a Northern Soul all-nighter so long ago I probably wouldn't remember were it not so damn memorable. He was stunning – a force of nature – the mod-est of all Motown mod icons. Little wonder that in later life he settled in Greater Birmingham to be close to the audience that appreciated and sustained him the most – British Mods and Northern Soul fans. So, having dragged about a dozen people along, including the de facto leader of the notorious Zulu Warriors hooligan gang, it was with a mixture of excitement and nerves that I approached this brand new soul club down one of Digbeth's half-secret side streets.

My trepidation was born of the feeling that NOBODY – not even his brother – could do justice to the crystal-clear vision of Edwin in my memory bank, but my fears were soon allayed. As the band struck up an infectious Northern groove, I was intently watching stage-right for a stereotypical soul-singer-style dramatic entrance. It was only when he leapt up out of the crowd and onto the stage that I realised that the well-dressed black man grooving along with the rest of us was in fact the Starr of the show. He grabbed the mic and roared, 'We came here to party!' – the cue for the band to launch into a string of Edwin's classic hits, including '25 Miles', 'Agent Double-O-Soul' and 'Stop her on Sight', greeted with near delirium by the crowd. This was an authentic soul band in an authentic soul venue and in a remarkable turnaround, people who attended the Stax-Volt revue could now be a little bit jealous of me!

The Team set fire to a host of standards like 'Get Ready' and 'Dancing in the Street', then Brummie Kev Kendall delivered a bassline only previously heard coming out of a Digbeth warehouse party to accompany a medley of 'Rapper's Delight', 'Good Times', 'Word Up' and 'Superstition', a sequence so funky that resistance to dancing was futile. Edwin's Wigan Casino monster 'Time' got a few Northern Soul snobs charging in from the beer garden, and they stayed on the dance floor for an incendiary rendition of worldwide number one hit 'War'. The Team left the stage to the kind of ovation I've rarely heard in a lifetime of gig-going after a great cover of Pharrell Williams' 'Happy' sent the crowd home erm … happy.

Finally, a word on the venue. The Night Owl is very more-ish – it's been open a month and I've been three times, and I don't get out much. It's a welcome addition to Brum's nightlife and there's a real friendly vibe about the place. Northern Soul has a lot in common with Birmingham, and Digbeth in particular. They're all cool, fun and undiscovered by the masses. Get down to the Night Owl and help change that.

UNIQUELY TALENTED

With the Night Owl acting as a magnet and a mid-life crisis that was going swimmingly well, I was being drawn into Digbeth on a weekly basis. I used to spend a lot of time in B5 as a young mod when they had nights at the Barrel Organ and Digbeth Civic Hall and had many a good night out there with my Zulu friends when I'd meet them after Birmingham City games. After a while, I began to notice a collective of brilliant young musicians who were very active in the area's nightlife, which inspired me to get tickets to one of their gigs.

Now, being a mod engenders an obsession about all kinds of black music, but this is not about race – it's all about the bass and a remarkable explosion of talent, bordering on a phenomenon, that, were it happening in Manchester, we'd never hear the last of. First of all, I heard a few episodes of the *Queen's Speech* series by Lady Leshurr at a fourth birthday party in Kingshurst, from where the Lady herself hails and, if anything, I was even more impressed than her young neighbours, who were all jumping around like House of Pain.

When I got home to the Wi-Fi, I checked out the videos and it was apparent that here was another star in Birmingham's remarkable 'great black female' firmament, worthy of taking her place alongside the likes of Joan Armatrading, Ruby Turner and Jaki Graham. The Queen of the Scene is musically very different from those fellow Brummies, but still part of an extraordinary group of contemporary black Birmingham females who threaten to equal the achievements of their B-Town predecessors. There's the seriously talented Laura Mvula, whose brilliant debut *Sing to the Moo*n was an epic album with a huge sense of scale and ambition.

More under the radar but making big waves is Mahalia, a 17-year-old who's already doing stuff like writing songs for Rudimental. Then there's a clutch of no less-talented artists like Jorja Smith, Stefflon Don, Truemendous, Sicnis, Lekky, Namywa, AffieJam and Lady Sanity, who are all well worth searching out.

Another is Call Me Unique, a young woman who has paid her dues in pubs, clubs and festivals, doing support slots, acoustic gigs and fronting a Hungarian jazz band (!). Her songs, full of great lyrics and hooks, have been honed to perfection over years of live performances. Her voice is tender and vulnerable one minute, soaring and savage the next, and always powerful, even when she sings in little more than a whisper. Strident, strong and vulnerable in equal parts, she sings, plays guitar, raps and scats – it's like Ella Fitzgerald grew up in Handsworth next door to Steel Pulse, listening to Amy Winehouse and The Streets.

So, with expectation building as I looked forward to seeing her live for the first time, I couldn't help thinking that this could be the perfect gig. First, the location is ideal – Birmingham is a city with a heritage of musical innovation and diversity that puts most others to shame, and by happy coincidence, it's also the hometown of tonight's star turn. Secondly, the venue itself ticks another box on my 'dream night out' list.

The Night Owl is the UK's only bespoke Northern Soul club, almost hidden down atmospherically urban Lower Trinity Street in Digbeth. Outside is the last word in industrial chic: clubs disguised as scrap metal yards, squeezed between heavy engineering works that double as canvasses for cutting-edge graffiti art. Inside, the vibe is seventies retro, yet somehow tasteful for all that.

Near neighbours include tech and creative hub, the Custard Factory, New Orleans-themed Mama Roux's, national rave treasure the Rainbow Venues, and the Old Crown, dispensing good beer and good cheer since 1368. So pre- and post-gig there's plenty to do to either warm up or wind down.

One thing that can always make or break a good night out is the company you're in, so the icing on the cake was persuading my wife to come along. She's probably bored rigid with me singing the praises of Unique, for which I can only apologise – but when I'm really into something I have an annoying habit of wanting to share it with anyone who'll listen.

CALL ME UNIQUE @ THE NIGHT OWL

As stage time approached, the band had all the ingredients simmering away nicely – now it was time for head chef Call Me Unique to bring everything to the boil. And man does she cook up a storm! Over the plaintive guitar that introduces opening number 'The Stranger', her voice is as clear as a bell. This is undoubtedly A Good Thing, as far from being superfluous, the lyrics are poetic and profound, and judging by the passion with which she delivers them, largely autobiographical. This is a woman who has suffered for her art, and the emotions given vent in the song 'Sholow' are so obviously raw, one almost feels guilty about being so enthralled and entertained by them.

Other songs have a defiant, militant edge, such as 'Bombs and Wars', a hard-hitting commentary on the futility of thug life. Hotly tipped local rapper Lady Sanity does an impromptu guest spot on this and doesn't put a foot or phrase wrong. Unique then lightens the mood with her anthem, 'The Wife', a jaunty tribute to womankind wherein she channels her inner India Arie and shows off her own rapping skills. Her versatility becomes apparent on house stomper 'Time to Love', which is well on the way to a couple of hundred thousand YouTube views, and she follows this up with a great version of the Destiny's Child hit 'Say my Name', which showcases the band's musicianship and Unique's stunning vocal dexterity.

Throughout the ninety-minute set, Unique quotes extensively from the encyclopaedia of black music, mixing a lethal cocktail of jazz, soul, hip-hop and RnB, all interspersed with between-song audience engagement which betrays a warm, open and humble personality – typical Brummie really. She's good. I mean Ella Fitzgerald, Amy Winehouse-type good. And only because I read a review saying that her fans tend to go 'a bit nutty' about her (guilty), I'm not comparing her to Nina Simone and Billie Holiday. Yet.

CALL ME UNIQUE. (© SOUL DIGGS)

SOUL MEN

Birmingham's urban music scene was beginning to bewitch me more and more, but I was still acting my age occasionally. I'd been in love with Tamla Motown since buying *20 Mod Classics Volumes 1 and 2* decades ago, and as Paul Weller once famously said on the Jonathan Ross show, 'I'm still a mod, I'll always be a mod, you can bury me a mod.' So the next gig was a no-brainer for me:

THE FOUR TOPS, THE TEMPTATIONS, TAVARES @ THE GENTING ARENA

My luck was in when I was at the park with the kids the other day. I got news of a spare ticket for a gig that should be on everyone's bucket list – the Temptations and the Four Tops, icons of America's motor city, playing in the original version – Birmingham. The Genting Arena is just a brisk walk followed by a one-stop train ride away from my home in the North Solihull stockbroker belt, so last minute though the call was, my attendance wasn't threatened by any major logistical problems.

Unfortunately, our Gang of Four couldn't get there in time to see the full set by support act Tavares, but on the plus side, we managed to catch their two biggest crowd-pleasers, 'More than a Woman' and 'Heaven Must be Missing an Angel'. Suitably warmed up, we took advantage of the break in proceedings to call a relative who works there on security and erm … secure seats a bit closer to the action.

The Tops and the Tempts have been touring together for decades, and while each band does their best to outshine the other, the rivalry is friendly enough for them to agree on taking it in turns to be headliners. Tonight the Temptations were first to take the stage, after a classic soul-style introduction from their veteran Master of Ceremonies.

Sharing the billing restricts their set to about an hour, which could never be sufficient for such a back catalogue, but it does guarantee a never-a-dull-moment intensity. Dance routines first taught by Motown choreographers fifty-odd years ago are as smooth as ever, and the songs are timeless. Sole surviving original member, Otis Williams makes a contribution that belies his 74 years, but the star of the show is undoubtedly Larry Briggs, whose voice stands up against any soul superstar I've seen – and I've seen a few. His fantastic vocals were to the fore on 'Ain't too Proud to Beg' and 'I Wish it Would Rain' – the composer of which committed suicide due to the heartbreak referred to in the song – then all the groups' talents were highlighted on a brilliant version of 'Ball of Confusion' and show-closer, introduced as 'our national anthem' – 'My Girl'.

Like the Temptations, the ravages of time have reduced the Four Tops to one original member – Abdul 'Duke' Fakir – and he wears his legendary status well. Duke does most of the talking and orchestrating, while his bandmates use their relative youth to recreate the power and energy of the dear, departed Levi Stubbs and Co. Highlights included 'Bernadette', 'Reach Out' and 'Standing in the Shadows of Love'. 'Simple Game' was simply great, and particularly poignant was 'The Same Old Song' – it has a different meaning with the others gone. 'I Can't Help Myself' was belted out ecstatically by the all-dancing crowd and crowned a fantastic evening. I'll definitely be getting tickets when this show's in town again, and I won't leave it so late next time.

GOD SAVE THE QUEEN

So, no change there then. I still loved the Tops and the Tempts. But in terms of my personal life, the next gig was revolutionary.

When I wrote the review the next day, sitting outside Café Rouge in the Bull Ring with a flat white and a packet of fags, the whole of Digbeth my vista, I glimpsed an alternate future – instead of labouring in a pallet depot, I saw myself sitting around town, smoking, drinking coffee and writing for a living. What a wonderful dream!

LADY LESHURR @ THE DIGBETH INSTITUTE

I plotted up at the Barrel Organ/Dubliner/Subside (depending on your age) where I had arranged to meet my two eldest sons Kurtis and Tyler. Heading straight to the smoking area, I got chatting to a well-refreshed black guy called Romeo who was rocking a pink Mohican haircut. When my boys arrived fashionably late, it turned out that Kurtis knew him. Well, we were in Birmingham – of course Kurtis knew him.

There were a few lads with guitars hanging around and I asked them who they were, to which they replied, 'The headliners are Drawstring, we're only the support act.'

'Yeah, what's your name?'

'You won't have heard of us.'

(This all-pervading Brummie humility can be annoying at times).

'Try me,' I said.

'Coffee Breath,' they replied, and it wasn't an observation, accurate though it may have been.

They were chuffed when I said I'd heard of and liked them and we stayed for the first bit of their set, which while a little rough around the edges was full of good ideas. We stayed partly because I wanted to hear them and partly because we wanted to avoid Leshurr's support act, Moka Blast. Sadly, we saw him, and he lived down to the review I'd read of a previous date. He came on in a balaclava as if trying to remain anonymous (I don't blame him), and his money gun broke again as I read it had in Liverpool the other night. He was rap's answer to Clinton Baptiste.

Mercifully Leshurr's DJ took over and warmed up the crowd with a string of classics from the likes of Outkast, Eve and Busta Rhymes and the joint was jumping. Not me, though, as I seemed to be being stalked by one of the Shurrcurity.

Our relationship had already got off to a bad start as I approached the venue, when he assumed by my greying sideburns that I might be at the wrong gig. Once inside, he moved me on from two or three excellent (if rather precarious) vantage points from which I had hoped to film proceedings on my phone, and eventually I had to settle for watching from the mayhem of the floor with the excitable proles who wouldn't stop jumping up and down in front of my camera.

Leshurr came on and started with the Sister Nancy cover 'Bam Bam', with frequent references to her home town Birmingham hyping the crowd up into a frenzy that never eased up. New song 'Mode' was well received and sounded up to the usual quality, then after 'Unleashed 2' she went off to get a royal-style robe and came back waving regally and accompanied by the national anthem.

She performed the first six *Queen's Speeches*, and although she rapped a fair bit of them, she didn't really need to as we sang most of the songs for her. She jumped into the crowd at one point, forgetting she was in Digbeth for a moment, and sure enough someone pinched her baseball cap. The Shurrporters were having none of it though and it was soon returned. She also got two fans up on stage to perform a rap battle to her biggest tune 'Queen's Speech 4' (61 million views on YouTube) and, thankfully, my sons' attempts to volunteer me were unsuccessful.

The devotion of the audience is quite something. Apart from all the bouncing around for which the beats can take the credit, there's the encyclopaedic knowledge of the lyrics, of which there are so many that learning them all is quite an achievement. I'm amazed SHE can remember them, never mind her fans. But they can, because they relate so closely, and this, for me, is the secret of her success. A non-believer might think her songs are just a series of put-downs and insults, but it goes much deeper than that. Because she does everything with such wit, charm, humility and warmth, her young audience is convinced she is on their side. It never enters their heads that she's blazing THEM – she is putting down that teacher you think treats you unfairly, your wasteman ex-boyfriend, your cheating ex-girlfriend, that crew of bullies making life hell at school. And she's doing it on YOUR behalf.

She might sound like a show-off if she wasn't so obviously genuine, but she is, so she doesn't. It was probably the most fun I've ever had at a gig, and I was grinning from ear to ear throughout. To top it off, she announced that she'd be waiting outside afterwards to chat and pose for selfies with anyone who wanted one. The queue was massive, made up of virtually everyone who had been in the gig, but about an hour and a half later, I finally got to meet her and she did a little video message for my 5 and 6-year-olds, Lewis and Amber, who love her. And this is why I love her too. I mean, I think she's great anyway – I love her flow, and I know lots of her clever and funny lyrics off by heart. She's also from my manor, so she's got absolutely everything going for her. But added to all that, she's a positive role model, a wonderful ambassador for Birmingham and she never swears or sings about sex, crime or drugs, which means my little kids and I can listen to her all day long with no worries at all, which we often and will continue to do.

PADDY AND STEVIE ... GONE TOO SOON

ALL OR NOTHING, THE MOD MUSICAL @ THE ALEXANDER THEATRE

I saw this show in London on its first run and enjoyed it so much I couldn't resist when it stopped off in Birmingham for a week. It tells the story of the rise and fall of ultimate mod band the Small Faces, taking in their eventful journey from London's East End via the boutiques of Carnaby Street to the top of the charts and on to their acrimonious break-up at the Alexandra Palace.

Aside from the classic theme of talent and ambition waylaid by sex, drugs and rhythm and blues, the show also exposes the band's exploitative management, both by Sharon Osbourne's dad, Don Arden (played menacingly here by Russel Floyd) and subsequently, Andrew Loog Oldham, who, having bought them out of a restrictive contract, should have made more of Marriott's brilliant singing and the sheer genius of his song-writing partnership with bassist Ronnie Lane. Stateside, in particular, they were never seriously promoted, yet a few years later the success of Humble Pie showed America's stadium-sized appetite for Marriott's voice and guitar virtuosity.

The songs are performed with great energy, and Samuel Pope acts and sings really well as the young Steve Marriott, although I doubt there's an actor alive who could do justice to his powerful, soulful vocals. It's understandable in a mod musical, but there's a touch too much of a particular mod obsession – attention to detail. So much happened in the band's four years together that it felt like fitting it all in was a tight squeeze. *Juke Box Jury*, Stanley Unwin, Sonny and Cher and Tony Blackburn cameos create nice comic relief, but I personally would welcome a bit more of the band's wonderful music.

Writer/producer Carol Harrison, who also plays a pivotal role as Marriott's mom, Kay, deserves credit for coming up with the idea of having a boozy, middle-aged Steve (Chris Simmons) almost permanently on stage as a ghostly narrator, explaining events for non-historians of the band and watching over his young self with a mixture of pride, embarrassment and caustic humour.

Simmonds' performance is the strongest in the show, but I'm probably biased as the real-life older Marriott was the one who I was acquainted with in the last few years of his life, when he seemed to enjoy the company of a few little mods coming down to London from Brum to idolise him every few weeks. I soon got to know Steve so well that, by the time he perished in a house fire in 1991, aged just 44, I owed him a fiver and he had my beloved vinyl copy of *Nina Simone Sings the Blues*.

We even met the various Ikettes who turned up at venues like the Half-Moon in Putney or the Queen's Head in Brixton. It's pretty mind-blowing for a young mod to be sitting in a boozer discussing your favourite records with the demi-god who actually made some of them, but when someone like Vanetta Fields (Google her) comes over, says hi and sits down at the same table ... well, I actually went dizzy.

Anyway, speaking of former Ikettes while somehow getting back to the show, Melissa Brown-Taylor almost steals it as Marriott's one-time lover, PP Arnold. Her a capella rendition of 'Angel of the Morning' gives rise to more goosebumps than anything else in the show bar the stripped-back, emotionally charged version of 'All or Nothing' that is part of a powerful and touching finale, before an uproarious singalong of all the hits. It's a great night out and highly recommended. None of my companions are obsessed with mod culture, in general, or the band in particular, like I am, yet they seemed to have just as good a time as me, albeit without the occasional tear that I shed for my old mate.

Post script: In the interval, while I was outside having a quick smoke, I saw my dear friend Paddy Dalton on the corner doing the same. It was the first time I'd seen him since, a few weeks previous, I'd bumped into him going into our local, the White Hart. He'd had his missus Kelly in tow and a card table under his arm and I asked him what was going on.

'It's a big poker tournament,' he explained. 'The early rounds are all in local pubs but if you get to the final it's on the telly and the top prize is a million pounds.'

'Are you playing bab?' I said to Kelly, but Paddy answered on her behalf. 'Yeah, yeah, she's playing, but really she's only here to make up the numbers.'

So, here we were outside the Alex a couple of weeks later and I asked him how he got on. 'Kelly won and knocked me out the bleedin' tournament didn't she!'

Paddy passed away recently in tragic circumstances ... another old mate to shed a tear for.

PARADISE IS TWICE AS NICE

LADY SANITY @ MAMA ROUX'S; NAMYWA @ THE HARE AND HOUNDS

It was Friday, it was pay day, my working week had finished, and the weather was as fresh and lovely as a Namywa vocal. Her gig at the Hare and Hounds – a support slot for new touring show 'Motown in Dub' that you can catch at this year's Simmer Down Festival in Handsworth Park – was scheduled to start at 10.30 p.m., so time was not pressing on me as I strolled around the quaint north Warwickshire hamlet of Chelmsley Wood, ice cream cone in hand, birds overhead singing melodies, reading my phone in the afternoon sun.

Then Twitter informed me that Lady Sanity was on at Mama Roux's at 6 p.m. as part of a Sound Lounge takeover of Digbeth Dining Club. This news put a spring in my step and added urgency to my hitherto relaxed stroll around the village shops. For a start, I had to run back to the bank to get the extra money needed for a longer night out, then collect the babbies from childcare and finally get into my wife's good books by cooking her dinner before dropping the 'I have to go out NOW!' bombshell.

It worked a treat and by five to six I was buying Sanity and her mom a drink at Mama Roux's in Digbeth's Lower Trinity Street, also home to Spotlight, the Night Owl, the Rainbow and Void, a new club set up in a derelict old monastery. Or did I dream that? Anyway, it's like Broad Street but with better music and cooler people.

Lady Sanity is a bit of a legend in these parts. A few weeks ago, I asked promoter Dragon Grime to name a Birmingham rapper destined for the top, and straight away he said, 'Sanity'. We then spent the next ten minutes talking about how great she is.

The undisputed queen of Brummie rap, Lady Leshurr gave her a shout out at her recent gig at the Digbeth Institute, and later on this evening, when Madi of Namywa's band asked, 'What was Sanity like?' I replied 'Brilliant', and Namywa herself interjected, 'She's *always* brilliant.'

Sanity opened with 'Future', typical of her sound in the way it promotes conscious and positive messages through reams of lyrics over old-skool hip-hop beats and jazzy brass and piano motifs. I'm loathe to pigeonhole her, but if you like A Tribe Called Qwest and The Pharcyde then chances are you'll like Sanity. She also looks the part with a 'fro to die for.

Other highlights include 'Blueprint', 'Bars for the Bin', 'Keep it Alive', 'When I'm Dreaming', 'The Pupil', 'Role Models' and the brilliant 'Kinda Funny' with its radio-friendly chorus. My personal favourite, though, is her hometown homage 'Yellow' – 'I got grey skyscrapers hanging over mine/About to paint the whole place until they see the shine/They see the metal/But never notice the petals'. There's so much information contained in her songs that if her debut album comes with a lyric book it will have to be sold in Waterstones in its own right. But it's quality AND quantity, the bars as profound as they are prolific.

If you're lucky enough to see her live, be prepared to concentrate. I was doing just that from my vantage point about 2 yards from the stage when an acquaintance came up to me and started a full-on conversation right in the middle of a song. I was abrupt enough to get rid of him, but that kind of thing must be frustrating for an artist like Sanity who pours her heart and soul into every performance.

After taking in a storming set by VSDN and thoroughly enjoying the stripped-back sound of Tehilla Henry, it was time to run the risk of crossing Digbeth High Street to catch the No. 50 to the Hare and Hounds.

Namywa started out by getting up on stage at an open-mic night a couple of years ago and stunning the crowd into silence with nothing more than a bit of spoken word. It was then she realised she might have something special. She turned her hand to song writing, and steady progress followed with the release of her *Garden of Eden* EP featuring the hard-hitting lyrics of 'F*** the Media' and 'The Beautiful One', which I immediately related to with its talk of a 'council estate kid' with 'drug dealers swimming round his feet'. And it wasn't just me – when I played it to my daughter, she described it as 'mesmerising'.

Namywa then stepped up a level with the launch of the *360 on Love* EP at the Sunflower Lounge. With drums and bass fleshing out her sound, songs we thought we knew became pulsating anthems. She had the look of a late-sixties Aretha and the stagecraft to match, and now I see her whenever I can.

She opened with the irresistible groove of 'Wound Up', a funky meandering stream of consciousness about old friends, ex-lovers and her determination not to be taken for a ride – unless it's on the No. 22 bus. Second song 'Stupid Me' is a story of unrequited love for a friend – 'You say it's not right/you say it's not time/whatever, that's fine/but you're a liar if you look at me/and say you don't see possibilities' – all wrapped up in classic soul. This was followed by 'Only the Sweetest', a real joy affair on which the chemistry between Namywa and (so much more than a) backing vocalist Madi Saskia casts an intricate, magical spell. In this, Namywa sings the phrase 'take a walk through my hypotheses' and somehow leaves it dripping with soul.

'Jungle' closes the show, a vibrant and uplifting roar for freedom from a restrictive relationship that showcases the talents of guitarist Ben, with Rochae driving it all along on bongos. So ruthless is her quality control that she could easily do an hour without a drop in standards, but it's the curse of the support act to have to cut short their set. That said, she could have been supporting Aretha Franklin and she'd still be the highlight for me. She's politically and socially aware, emotionally articulate and mature and a great singer. It's early days yet but she has enough songs for an amazing debut album and if I win big on the lottery this weekend, I swear I'm going to fund the recording and promotion of it myself.

LADY SANITY. (© LEE CRAWFORD, DISTORTED IMAGE PHOTOGRAPHY)

BLINDED BY THE NIGHT

It's not just music that makes Birmingham great ...

PEAKY BLINDERS TOUR @ THE OLD CROWN AND VARIOUS OTHER DERITEND LOCATIONS

I was going to start by saying that I'm in Digbeth so often I might as well move there, but I found out last night that it is actually Deritend where I spend most of my nights out. Know the difference? Me neither, but this was just one of many facts I discovered on the Peaky Blinders tour, booked for me as a Father's Day gift by my thoughtful wife Kerri and coinciding with her dad Trevor's birthday.

The starting point is the Old Crown on the high street at seven o'clock, and I make it just in time after entering into the spirit of things by not paying on the train to town. If you like the TV show, you'll love this tour, but it covers so much more than the blurred lines of fact and fiction of the popular BBC period drama.

Convivial as ever, our host, tour guide, author, historian, professor and raconteur, Carl Chinn takes us on a journey that begins in 1880s Birmingham and meanders between two world wars, back to the origins of the city and forward to the infamous 2002 face-off between the Aston Villa Hardcore hooligan gang and their Birmingham City counterparts, the Zulus. Known to modern-day weekend offenders as the Battle of Rocky Lane, from now on I'll think of it as Rocky Lane II, as we learn that a previous massive gang fight took place on the very same spot around a century earlier. Sadly, only the more recent tear-up is available on a dodgy DVD.

After a splendid introduction from his assistant Lizzie Halpin, who's Uncle John has been known to keep the odd Peaky Blinder tradition going in the twenty-first century, Carl delivers a sparkling prelude in which he goes from guest to guest giving them historical chapter and verse on wherever it is they come from. Tonight's party includes people from Switzerland, Worcester, Yorkshire, Rhode Island, Evesham, Lebanon, Tipton and my lot from Handsworth, and Carl's encyclopaedic knowledge bats away questions on each and every location with the ease of Arthur Shelby dealing with a stroppy bookmaker. With considerably more charm and grace, obviously.

Pre-amble over, we start on the actual amble – the walking tour. This is fascinating, taking in the site of some long gone back-to-back houses and courtyards, a beautiful Italianate monastery (now home to rave club Void), Brum's first free library, and legendary pub the Rainbow, where an incident in 1890 led to the first mention of the Peaky Blinders in the newspapers of the day.

Carl paints such a vivid picture of this 'murderous assault' that the sudden appearance of a couple of Peakied-up gangsters round the corner in Lower Trinity Street might make you check the inside pocket of your crombie to make sure your cosh is handy. Or was that just me? Anyway, the presence of the menacing hardmen under the magnificent Staffordshire blue-brick railway arches is an ideal photo opportunity and many of the tourists take full advantage.

As Carl shares his extensive knowledge of the lives and times of our gangster predecessors, it's very much a two-way exchange, and he is always open to questions and comments from his enrapt charges. One amusing moment occurs when a young Swiss girl asks my mother-in-law Carmen, who is of West Indian descent, how she knows so much about Birmingham, and seems rather confused when Carmen explains that she was born and bred in the city. The moral of this story is: never presume to know what a native Brummie looks like. Start from the premise of the old joke on how to tell a true Brummie – he always wears a shamrock in his turban – and you won't go far wrong. (Yes, I know that was originally a racist joke and a dig at Birmingham all rolled into one, but we who celebrate our unrivalled diversity own it now, so there.)

As someone who spends lots of weekend nights on these streets, it's striking how different the vibe is on a Tuesday evening. An unusually sober view of the architecture and graffiti and the absence of revellers, bouncers and taxi headlights make it seem a lot moodier, and I would love to do this tour again when the nights start to draw in, to feel the full effect of the darkness. I imagine it would be quite haunting and oppressive – but in a good way, given the subject matter.

With an affectionate glance towards the Night Owl as we pass, it's time to head back to the Old Crown, where pre-ordered drinks await us at our tables – mine's a pint of Peaky Blinder, cheers! – and we settle down again to listen to Carl's wonderful storytelling and insight. I won't spoil it for you with details, but this is where the eminent historian really comes into his own. Speaking from painstaking research, hand-me-down anecdotes and first-hand experience, Carl's passion and love for 'Brummagem' and its people comes shining through. It's eloquent, entertaining and emotional and rounds off a cracking night perfectly. I can't recommend it highly enough, so book yourself a place on the tour – by order of the Peaky Blinders!

AMONGST BUTTERFLIES

In between gigs, I took up interviewing some of my favourites. In this one, Swim Deep prodigy, The New Consistent, talked about life, love, transparent butterflies and BBQs with Wolf Alice.

When JAWS frontman Connor Schofield recently gave me a rundown of local artists he thought were making moves and doing bits, it was mostly a case of the usual suspects. Sugarthief, Ivory Wave, Riscas and The Assist are quite well known to Midlands music enthusiasts, and if they're not, they should be.

One name on his list, The New Consistent, was new to me, so I fired up the search engine to check them out. I discovered an EP called *Individual Social Accounts and Commentary*, produced by Swim Deep's Ozzy Williams; five slices of post-millennial relationship narrative – and a video for the song 'Rude Boys'. The sound is a sort of low-fi, downbeat mixture of The Streets, Swim Deep and a more reflective, less angry Sleaford Mods, and the video is the kind of thing Shane Meadows might come up with. I was intrigued enough to search out their driving force, 19-year-old Ben Ramsay, to find out more …

How did you link up with Ozzy?

It was a weird one actually. I sent him a demo of mine and he ended up loving it and we got chatting for ages. He kind of took me under his wing and ended up producing most of my EP. I went down to his in London to record it, and we went to a barbecue with Wolf Alice. Very surreal.

I don't know what came first, but I can hear your style on Swim Deep's comeback single 'To Feel Good'. Do you think maybe you influenced it a bit?

Yeah, a few people mentioned it to me when it came out. I think so, but it wasn't talked about between me and Oz. It is what it is though, if I did influence it then it's a compliment to me, I guess. Good tune though, a great one to mark their comeback with.

I take it you're a fan?

Yeah of course. I think every kid in Brum is to be fair!

I read that you're from Worcester. How come you ended up in Birmingham?

I'd lived in Brum, Acocks Green, for seven years with my family before we moved to Worcester, then I came back because of my girlfriend and my mates living in and around the city. I'd always been going to gigs in Brum, though, because Worcester is so close.

A similar journey to Peace.

Yeah. I think Doug and Dom went to the same sixth form as me actually. Dom's old man was the vicar of a church round the corner from my old house.

How and when did you get into making music?

I'd been doing demos since I was 14 just on my phone, then it developed as I got older. I was 17 when I first started to write seriously though. '3 Years' was my first proper song. The demo of it is still on my soundcloud, and that's the first vocal take I ever did!

There's one song on your first EP – 'Greta Oto' – that sounds like it might be about some obscure European actress. So, who is Greta Oto?

Haha, no! It's actually the scientific name for a butterfly with transparent wings – I had to Google it – and I felt as though a butterfly with see-through wings limits itself in its beauty and is a limited butterfly in general, but obviously it can't help it cos that's just the way it is. And I saw that as a metaphor for me and my mate who the song is about. Our friendship is limited and can never always be good or beautiful because of the natural limitations or problems that my mate has, that will never change. It means a lot, that song. I think everyone's got that mate that they're more like family with, and therefore you go through stages where you're so close, then fall out and don't speak for a while, and it just continues forever.

You use your own accent. Was that ever in doubt?

I was never gonna try and be something I'm not, I couldn't imagine the stick I'd get if I tried anything otherwise.

Obviously, I know Swim Deep's sound and I'd pick up on that vibe even if I didn't know Oz was involved, but who else influences you?

Well, there's a few and to be honest since the first EP dropped my sound has shifted slightly and become more of a solid style. Musically, I'm influenced by Jorja Smith, Loyle Carner, Rejjie Snow, and lyrically probably The Rhythm Method and maybe Alex Turner, as well as Loyle Carner again.

Where does the name come from?

It was originally a lyric in my debut single. While that was getting mixed, me and Ozzy were brainstorming names cos I was struggling to think of one. His girlfriend said, 'What about The New Consistent?' after she'd heard the song, and it just stuck. In the song it kind of represented my new life that I'd found. I'd just come out of a three-year relationship that I'd been in since I was 15, and so was experiencing life as a whole different thing, which is what that song is about, and so it summed up my new life. Coincidentally, music started happening around the same time, which made me feel as though The New Consistent was meant to be.

'Rude Boys' isn't on the EP. Is it the start of a new project?

Yeah, it is. It kind of bridges the gap between the first and second EPs. Like I said before, the new stuff is me finding my sound and my style, so 'Rude Boys' is leading people into that. It got a good reaction which is promising!

It's a promise that The New Consistent has been fulfilling ever since.

A UNIQUE NIGHT OUT

I was back in Digbeth for the next one, watching the unique Unique conducting a cast of dozens at the launch party for her new EP. Every now and again, I have a night out in Birmingham I know I'll never forget, and this was one of them.

CALL ME UNIQUE AND FRIENDS @ MAMA ROUX'S, DIGBETH

I knew it would be good – one glance at the line-up told me that – and my eagerness to get started meant my son Tyler and I were enjoying the heavy rock and hospitality at Subside a good couple of hours before showtime. But it took longer than a Led Zeppelin guitar solo to get served, so it was lucky we allowed plenty of time.

'Is it because I'm a mod?' I asked the long-haired, tattooed barman.

'No,' he said, looking me up and down with barely concealed contempt. 'I'm just busy.'

The band in there (sound of Slipknot, look of the Inbetweeners) weren't really my thing, so I hastily rearranged the meet with my mate Lee to the altogether more civilised surrounds of the Old Crown, where we sank a couple of pints of Peaky Blinder and headed for the venue, just round the corner in Lower Trinity Street.

What a vibe! Digbeth Dining Club was heaving as always, and though the aromas drifting into the courtyard of Mama Roux's were very tempting, the mouth-watering on-stage menu ensured that no amount of pulled pork and dirty burgers could drag me away. The first half of the show consisted of Unique and her incredibly tight band performing her first EP, aided and abetted by a host of talented local artists. On haunting opener 'The Stranger', Unique was joined by rappers Trademark Blud and The Boy October, the first two links in a chain of collaborators with not a single weak link.

Next up, the sensual tones of Kezia Soul and Simon Jnr turned up the heat on slow burner 'Here', a song so sexy it should come with an 18 certificate. Then came two of Birmingham's most accomplished MCs, RTKAL, who gave probably the best performance I've ever heard on Radio 1xtra's *Fire in the Booth*, and Lady

Sanity. If she were to appear on Charlie Sloth's show, he would be well advised to have the actual fire brigade on speed dial. They joined Unique for 'Urban Gypsy', the title track of her first EP, and as the two of them went bar for blistering bar, the appreciative crowd began to get really hyped.

Jugganaut and Malik MD7 did absolutely nothing to calm the mood as they put their own slant on the gritty and uncompromising 'Bombs and Wars', Jugganaut combining the authoritative voice of a reanimated Biggie Smalls with the energy of Beanie Man, while Malik reprised his pivotal performance on the recorded version of the song, this time with even more fire and skill.

Thankfully, for the old mod in the audience, things calmed down as the first half of the show was brought to a close by the raw emotion of Sholow, backed by the soaring falsetto of local hero Ed Geater and what I expected to be the beautifully delicate voice I know and love from AffieJam's recorded output. I was pleasantly surprised to hear that voice transformed into a soulful tour de force in a live setting, and no sooner had I got my breath back than she took it away again.

After a short interval, Unique resigned from her first-half role as convivial host coaxing all these wonderful performances from her mates and took centre stage. She opened with a storming cover of 'Genie in a Bottle', then the focus shifted to the new EP. Following the lovely folk-tinged 'Birds', she showed off her rapping credentials on 'The Only Girl in Manville', cleverly co-opting the chorus from Grandmaster Flash's 'The Message' and followed this up with a fantastic version of the Destiny's Child hit 'Say my Name', featuring the sultry vocals of jazz chanteuse Tina Amana ripping it up alongside the headliner. The band really excelled on this, and the New Orleans theme of the venue was a perfect setting for the funkiest combo this side of the Big Easy.

The final guest of the second half was Leanne Louise, who's rich, bluesy voice was used to stunning effect on 'H###tag', After the obligatory, crowd-pleasing outing of celebratory anthem 'The Wife', it was back to the new stuff. Lead single from the EP, 'Shoulda' , is an absolute banger, the dark lyrics telling of domestic violence, carried along by a relentless, driving beat. The *pièce de résistance*, though, is both the EP and the show's closer, 'Ashon'. This is a fragile paean to Unique's unborn son, who tragically passed away, that through its sheer humanity somehow turns out to be the most life-affirming moment of the show.

The whole evening was a showcase for the incredible number of accomplished artists we are truly blessed to have right here on our doorstep in Birmingham. I was lucky enough to meet lots of them on the night, as well as Unique's lovely family, and their modesty and humility was as obvious as their talent. If some of the names are new to you, please check them out, and maybe you'll be there next time. You won't regret it.

BRING IT ON, MANCHESTER

Disclaimer: If any Shotty fans are reading this, welcome to Birmingham. Just so you know … my kids and the second city are the stars of this review – your boy may get the odd mention and a few lines at the end if he was any good, capeesh?

SHOTTY HORROH, CITYLIGHTZ, PAGANS S.O.H., BLUE NATION @ THE HARE AND HOUNDS, KINGS HEATH

After years of dragging my kids out to watch my heroes, the tables turned when they told me they had eight tickets to see theirs. Shotty Horroh has few peers in the battle rap scene that my nippers love so much, and it is no surprise that he has graduated from that school of hard knocks to become a fully fledged Rock Star.

I wasn't that keen at first – Shotty's a Manc for a (bad) start, and I would need to book time off work – but when I heard that Wolverhampton's Citylightz were on the bill, I was in the gaffer's office filling in a holiday form like I was claiming a cash prize.

I'd normally start by saying that Kirsty, Kurtis and Tyler met Dad in town, but given the subject of the review it seems appropriate to use our battle rap names. So, Loxy, Penance and Tydal met Old Father Grime at the No. 50 bus stop outside Selfridges and the condensed madness began.

An incoherent, under-the-influence woman seemingly offered Tydal an unopened block of cheese as we boarded the Hare and Hounds Express (the bus) and, after declining her offer with his usual impeccable manners – he's a grime clasher, not a gangster rapper – he sat down with the rest of us in the seats behind her. We were laughing and joking about something completely unrelated, when cheese woman turned round and said, 'Keep laughing at me, see what happens.'

Concerned about this thinly veiled, although not particularly terrifying, threat towards me and my children, I asked her to expand on her concerns. She proceeded to complain that Tydal had refused her request to open her cheese.

Realising his mistake, he obliged – luckily, he was packing his shank (kidding) – and Cheddar Barb had polished off the whole block before we'd travelled a mile, never mind eight. Drama, drama, what a palaver!

We alighted at the Hare to find Fungi out of Benefits Street at his usual pitch in the pub's smoking area, and he gave me the look that he always does, a sort of enigmatic half-smile that says, 'Yes, it IS me'. I know Fungi, how could I forget? And no, I don't want a *Big Issue*.

After getting my hand stamped by the doorman (Liam out of Brum indie wunderkind, The Clause), we went in to check out the opening act, Blue Nation. They were having to do an acoustic set as their drummer got run over the night before – true story – but the way they were taking the micky out of him, it couldn't have been too serious.

The former trio, now a duo, were modded-up in Paisley button-down shirts and asked the crowd to put our hands up if we thought they were an Oasis tribute act. Some wag shouted, 'Do Wonderwall!' and that kind of spoiled things for me because, from then on, the start of every tune they did sounded like the opening of 'Wonderwall'. Even 'Champagne Supernova' (I'm joking).

SHOTTY HORROH. (© PHIL DRURY, 2324 PHOTOGRAPHY)

I'm not sure if it's a pro or a con, but when you go to this sort of gig, the presence of a lot of wannabe rappers in the audience means the blazing area outside is often as entertaining as the gig – full of MCs spitting bars and doing cyphers (standing round in a circle taking turns at rapping), not to mention the smell of green. It's great fun, but the drawback is you lose out on seeing some good support acts.

I missed most of the Pagans S.O.H. set due to this, but fortunately I did catch my favourite tune of theirs, 'Banananah', with which they closed their set. It's a great song and they performed it brilliantly. Then it was a back outside for a smoke, a slurp and another cypher. This time, even Fungi joined in with the verbal parring and sparring – he really is a fun guy! Sorry kids – shame on your father.

I didn't hang about outside for long as Shotty had brought the Manchester weather with him and the fantastic CityLightz were up next, tearing through a five-song white knuckle ride of a set. Opening with new single 'Proof', they finished with a pair of aces, anti-police anthem 'Piggy', and the story of the Black Country's own Keyser Soze, 'Tim'. Yeah, you read it right, a gangster called Tim, short for Timothy. I'd get an evil nickname if I were him.

Shotty and I nearly bumped into each other downstairs as his minder led him through a back way to the stage. 'Sorry fella,' he said, and his good manners had already got him in my good books. First impressions got even more favourable when he spent his first minute on stage singing Birmingham's praises, before launching into opening number 'Shudehill' – 'I was in Shudehill, City won 2–0'. He followed this up with the excellent 'Danger', and I was a bit worried at this point as he'd started with the only two songs of his I knew. I needn't have worried. Following the single 'Dirty Old Town', he ripped through the rest of his debut album *Salt of the Earth* and the quality never dipped. I'll be buying that soon.

He threw in an accomplished cover of the Arctic Monkeys' 'Fake Tails of San Francisco', followed by 'Dynamite', which bangs, obvs, and also performed one from his next album, 'Especially You'. If that is anything to go by, I'll go buy that one too. Have I got bars or what?

The between-song banter was top quality, and at one point he asked if there were any Villa fans in the audience (big cheer), then Blues (smaller cheer and some embarrassed shuffling). Although I shouted my head off at my cue, I couldn't help but worry, as the last time I heard the crowd being split along those lines was by the DJ in Rumours social club in Chelmsley Wood, and it led to a near riot and about fifteen life bans.

Shotty is backed by a powerful, all-Canadian band – lead and rhythm guitars, bass and drums – and they bring his recorded music stunningly to life. The man himself is a fantastic frontman, oozing the swagger of Liam Gallagher if he drank in the Jockey, singing lyrics Alex Turner would be proud of, and pinging around the stage with the energy of the pre-heroin Libertines. He finished with a triptych (look it up Brexiters) of great songs – 'Wish You Well', 'Lanyards' and 'Stay for the Ride' – before telling us we were the best audience of the tour and immediately joining his fans for complicated handshakes, hugs and selfies.

I can't believe I doubted him. He said he'd been dying to come to 0121 and tear the roof off – he delivered, and I hope he does again. I can't thank Tydal enough for sorting my ticket and him, Loxy and Penance for their wonderful company.

I was on cloud nine all day the next day with 'Danger' like a twenty-four-hour virus in my ears – until I came down to earth with a bump on Friday night. I was near Spring Hill, Villa lost 3–0.

HAPPY BIRTHDAY TO ME!

PAUL WELLER @ GENTING ARENA; PEACE @ GODIVA FESTIVAL; LADY SANITY @ THE FLAPPER

Hey Shorty, it's my birthday, and over the course of eight days I had tickets to see Paul Weller at the Genting Arena, a table for dinner and a hotel stay in my favourite city in the world, hippie icons Peace playing at the Godiva Festival in Coventry, and Lady Sanity live on the last leg of a nationwide tour.

The first instalment went well, although I nearly aborted the Weller gig by returning my tickets due to the unbearable lateness of being paid monthly. It was only while I was on hold waiting for my refund to be confirmed that the full horror of missing my life coach playing ten minutes from my yard hit home, and I ended up withdrawing the money I got back for two tickets and exchanging it for one off a tout. The bloke who was supposed to be going with me wasn't impressed but maybe he'll organise it all next time.

I ended up popping my head into Zulu HQ (the White Hart in Tile Cross), where there are always a few people plotting up when Weller is in town, and cadging a lift off one of my Blues mates, Paul Caffrey, and his missus Courtney. They're not all bad. I asked Our Court if Paul had infected her with his irrational hatred of the Villa, and while she was thinking of a tactful answer, he interrupted, 'I wouldn't say it's irrational.'

I'm really glad I had a change of heart about going. From the opening riff of 'White Sky' to the absolute scenes that greeted 'A Town Called Malice', the whole gig was a thunderous triumph, covering almost every aspect of his forty-odd years of making beautiful music. While the Guvnor is starting to look his age, his enthusiasm for live performance remains undimmed, his voice is better than ever and the next album (his twenty-sixth!) promises to be a masterpiece.

The next day, me and Wifey's romantic dinner and hotel stay at the Mailbox was lovely, but if you think I'm reviewing that you've got another think coming. Suffice it to say that while I'm starting to look my age, my enthusiasm for live performance remains undimmed. And no, I haven't got an album coming out.

On to the next weekend and seeing Peace for the first time. I'm still kicking myself that, years ago, I missed one of their earliest gigs by preferring to stand outside smoking and drinking while they played in a little Birmingham boozer called the Adam and Eve. I vaguely recall guitarist Doug Castle coming out and ordering a rag-tag collection of disinterested fag-heads inside to watch them, telling us that his band were 'better than the Beatles'. I told him that I didn't like the Beatles and stayed outside. My loss.

I was a bit more eager to see their appearance at this year's Godiva Festival at Coventry's War Memorial Park. I liked the band's first two albums, but I absolutely love their latest, *Kindness is the New Rock and Roll*, and it's probably the first album since Weller's *Stanley Road* that I can sing to myself all the way through while pottering about at the pallet depot.

Packed full of great tunes, clever lyrics and anthemic choruses, it also conveys a message of love and peace that really is what the world needs now. Such was my enthusiasm, I was listening to the former Digbeth night-life regulars via the aux in my wife's car as she dropped me off at Marston Green station. The Coventry train was at the platform as we pulled up and I unplugged my phone and jumped aboard.

It was only as we moved off that I realised that the phone, now in my pocket, was still playing 'Lovesick' from the band's debut album. As I retrieved it to turn it off (I'm not 12 and hate it when I'm forced to listen to other people's invariably awful music on public transport), a few of my fellow passengers joined in with the chorus. I was encouraged to play further requests and the impromptu Peace karaoke continued all the way to Cov.

I arrived at the park an hour before the band were due on stage, spotted a gap along the fence right at the front and claimed it. I was thirsty, but not thirsty enough to give up this prime spot, so I put out a hopeful message online for somebody to bring me a drink. I soon felt a hand on my shoulder and turned around to the welcome sight of my mate, a performance poet and fully qualified archbishop, standing there with a much-appreciated pint of lager. How generous and intrepid!

Peace took the stage to loud cheers and started with a lively 'Lovesick' that got the huge crowd straight into it, then followed up with the new album's opening track 'Power'. 'I'll whisper in your ear/I'll swallow all your fear/I can lick my lips and make the darkness disappear,' sang Harry, and I for one believed him. 'Money' and 'Lost on Me', two tracks from their second album *Happy People*, had the crowd roaring back the lyrics, and then I admit I got a bit sentimental over 'California Daze', which I interpret as a paean to Zombie Prom nights at the Rainbow, days in the Pigeon Park, and that ex-girlfriend you can't get out of your head. We've all got one, haven't we?

Then it was back to the new stuff with the riff-tastic 'You don't Walk Away from Love' and the emotional 'Magnificent'. The mosh pit was in full effect for 'Bloodshake' and 'Wraith' before the more reflective 'From Under Liquid Glass' (Francis Bean Cobain's favourite song of the decade) closed the show. Roll on Digbeth Institute in November.

I was back on home turf the next night as Erdington MC Lady Sanity ended her nationwide tour with a sell-out show at the Flapper. I had ten tickets for this one as I won't rest until everyone I know realises just how brilliant she is.

I caught the train at Marston Green again, this time travelling to New Street, with text messages pinging between cousins, friends and my kids as I organised pick-up points and directions. It was a bit of a culture clash between the various branches of my family tree – some of them were well turned out and wanted to meet outside the Brasshouse in Broad Street. Then we had to link with the rest of them, for whom every day is dress-down day, at the little park at the back of the library, where they were blazing weed in the dark. It took a while to find them, but in the end, I just followed my nose and we eventually teamed up.

We got to the venue in time to see all four supporting acts, with Sanity warmly introducing each one and giving them all a big build-up. They were all enjoyable and undoubtedly talented, but when the Lady herself took the stage things moved up to another level. Opening with 'They Won't Hear a Word', she had the home crowd on-side straight away. This was followed by 'Role Models', which built into a crescendo of hype bars and the whole room bouncing up and down to the chorus.

Sanity split the crowd into two sets of backing singers for the next track, a cover of Tupac's 'Do for Love', and she finished with the fantastic 'Fro'z', after which there was prolonged cheering, followed by everyone in the room chanting her name and forcing her back on stage for an impromptu cover of Kendrick Lamar's 'Humble'. She's so modest, she looked embarrassed. Her lyrics throughout were profound, conscious, intelligent and inspirational, and as I said to the camera crew who collared me after the show, she might not be the best rapper in the country, but she's definitely in the top one.

So, for my birthday this year I saw great gigs from acts who, at first glance, don't seem to have much in common. It's true that they vary widely in age and genres but look a little deeper and it strikes me that Weller, Peace and Sanity all have a positive message that the world needs to hear, and all three delivered with a level of skill and conviction rarely matched in modern music. More power to them.

WE ARE FAMILY

MADI SASKIA AND FRIENDS @ THE HARE AND HOUNDS

Families can be complicated, can't they? Children don't always follow the path you do your best to map out for them. Some of mine aren't bothered about football, for instance, although they know better than to say they're anything other than Villa fans. No one wants to be disinherited after all.

Still, constant screenings of the Eminem film *8 Mile* in my house when they were growing up helped turn three of them into accomplished and witty wordsmiths, so keep your eyes and ears peeled for the music and rap battles of Loxy, Penance and Tydal on an internet platform near you. Their little brother and sister are, at 6 and 7 years old respectively, a bit young for grime clashes, but they still contribute to my night out by squirting toothpaste into the shoes I was going to wear. Bless 'em.

Every single year their mom, my wife, has the temerity to have her birthday the day after Valentine's Day. Not only does this lead to the postman thinking she's a woman of questionable morals, it often curtails my gig-going, review writing and football attendance. Tonight's volunteer to throw a family-shaped spanner in the works is middle son Tydal, who I'm supposed to meet in town. When I ring him, he's near the Square Peg and I'm waiting at Digbeth Coach Station. Twenty minutes later, I'm still waiting. I ring him in a bit of a parental panic, thinking that he must have been mugged or something, only to find that he's way over the other side of Digbeth in Fazeley Street. See what I mean about children not following the right path?

Anyway, he finally turns up un-mugged but carrying about as much cash as if he had been, and we walk round the corner to the No. 50 bus stop, heading for the legendary Hare and Hounds. Another family-related problem occurs when Madi Saskia's dad, on door duties, takes some convincing that I've come to the right show. I had the same problem at my last Lady Leshurr gig – I'm obviously getting a bit long in the tooth for this malarkey. Tydal is a bit starstruck when he sees Lady Sanity in the crowd and is even more impressed to discover that she and I are on first-name terms as I give her a fist bump and say, 'Hello Lady'. It makes a nice change for me to go out and see someone who doesn't only recognise me as my kids' dad, although that does happen later when I saw the talented and lovely singer Janel Antonesha in the blazing area – I also met local legend Lekky at last and she was absolutely lovely, too.

This is like being backstage at Live Aid for me, only better because U2 aren't here. There's a procession of impressive supporting acts, including poet Adjei and rappers Jiggs, D-Tox, Amiri and Yosei, followed by singer Reeceyboi and his beautiful dancers, and finally some intense and moving poetry from Aliyah Denton. The family theme is continued when I discover later that Yosei went to college with my sister-in-law, Olivia.

Madi took the stage looking as stunning as ever and with a couple of dancers in tow and won the crowd over without singing a note via some great choreography. She began her set proper with 'Rainbows', showing justified confidence in her own song-writing skills. Then came the first in a series of imaginative and brilliantly executed covers, as she gives us her sensual reading of Jhene Aiko's 'The Worst'.

Similarly well suited to the headliner's style was a fantastic mash-up of Kehlani's 'Gangsta' and Blu Cantrell's 'Breathe', with the excellent Jabez Walsh reimagining the Sean Paul bits. Usually a percussionist in Namywa's band, Rochae takes on a more prominent role tonight on backing vocals, and further proves her versatility when performing her own song, 'Life', complete with enthusiastic audience participation. This is followed by a couple more Madi originals, 'Saw you First' and 'Tell me What we're Smoking', the appeal of which is apparent on first listen, and is one of the highlights of the set. If you're reading Madi, please upload this song ASAP!

Ms Saskia is then joined by my long-time soul heroine Namywa and the aforementioned Lekky on 'Four White Walls', 'Find your Way out' and Namywa's anthem 'Jungle', and I'm simultaneously nodding my head to the beat and shaking it in disbelief at how all this talent has only cost a fiver to witness.

Guitarist Ben Jones comes to the fore on a blistering cover of Cardi B's 'Bodak Yellow', and the show is brought to a close with a couple more of the star turn's own songs, the beautiful 'F.O.O.L.S' followed by Madi effortlessly turning up the vocal power on the storming 'Runnin'', with the hyped crowd joining in on the hook.

Throughout the hour-long show, the band and the various rappers and singers create a real feel-good vibe, and here is why I've been banging on about 'family' throughout this piece: this collective of musicians, including bassist George Foley, drummer Ashley Lawson and Jamael Jarrett on keyboards, can often be seen at each other's shows, all contributing what they're good at (which is plenty), supporting one another and inspiring each other to greater artistic heights.

They put on a great show and I leave with a warm glow and the lasting impression that they're one big, happy family. It's a genuine pleasure and privilege to see.

PEACE OFFERING

Coronation Street in the morning, Digbeth High Street on the night …

PEACE @ DIGBETH INSTITUTE

I spend most of my leisure time seeking out new Birmingham music on the internet, but until quite recently Peace had passed me by. I liked the first two albums but didn't love them. I heard Radio One say they were 'The Sound of 2013' and read in the *Guardian* that they were the future of indie, but for some reason I wasn't convinced. Nothing they did quite grabbed me like their mates Swim Deep did with 'King City', the signature tune of the B-town scene.

Peace seemed to disappear from my radar completely after the second album, *Happy People*, and my mate said he saw one of the boys in Snobs who'd told him they were 'taking a break'. I thought they were finished, and though I was a bit sad, I wasn't inconsolable.

I had my first real moment of clarity re: Peace when I heard 'From Under Liquid Glass', released in support of mental health charity MQ and, like Kurt Cobain's daughter Francis Bean, I loved it. It signalled a new maturity in Harry Koisser's song-writing and sparked an interest in their third album, *Kindness is the New Rock and Roll*. I overcame long-standing Luddite tendencies to buy it as a digital download, and then bought the physical CD hoping for a lyric sheet (sadly missing). I also bought the first two albums, and soon, as you do with children, I grew to love them all the same.

A spur-of-the-moment jaunt to Coventry to see them at the Godiva Festival confirmed I was becoming obsessed with the band in a way I'd not been since following the Style Council around on a UK tour for an entire month back in the eighties, when I didn't have a wife and six kids to worry about. When I bought tickets to see them at the Digbeth Institute, I also had a week in Mexico and a trip to my beloved Coronation Street to look forward to, but they became mere hurdles on the way to Peace's glorious homecoming.

The Corrie tour, on the morning of the gig, was great, and helped get me through what would otherwise have been a tortuous wait for the main event. I took loads of photos of me and Wifey outside the knicker factory (Manchester's greatest contribution to British manufacturing), and Roy's Rolls, 0161's best hope for a Michelin star, but remained distracted. On the drive home I broke into a cold sweat at every sign of potential traffic jams, and at around Stafford I put on my seatbelt in the back, so determined was I to stay alive until after the gig at least.

I made it home safe, and barely had time to say hello to the cat before I was Birmingham-bound with a mate who I bumped into at Marston Green station. I told him I was going to see the best live band in the world, and he informed me that 'The Clash have split up, mate'. He was on his way to see a Clash tribute act at the Asylum and on any other night I'd have been sorely tempted.

I met up with future grime star Penance in town, and just when I thought things couldn't get any better, we bumped into AffieJam (full title, The Very Wonderful Musician And Blogger AffieJam) in the boozer next door to the venue and we exchanged cider and pleasantries before heading to the Institute. The stars were aligning – Birmingham's coolest man and woman (Harry and Affie) would soon be in the same building. Thank God I wore plenty of layers.

The band took the stage to thunderous applause and announced their arrival with an appropriate cover of Thin Lizzy's 'The Boys are Back in Town'. Following a powerful rendition of latest album opener erm … 'Power', the band switched between their three long-players at will, performing 'Money' from the second and 'Toxic' from their debut, before treating us to the magnificent 'Magnificent', and the riff-laden 'You don't Walk Away from Love'. 'Flirting USA' and the Who-like power chords of 'Lost on Me' preceded the beautiful and heartfelt 'Silverlined', my go-to song in those moments when, to quote the lyrics, 'Life comes down on me with all its devilry'.

It was indie dance floor time again as 'Perfect Skin' and 'I'm a Girl' were given an airing, the latter a number I'd been particularly looking forward to for the line 'When I was in Digbeth I felt so alone'. After a haunting cover of Nine Inch Nails' 'Hurt', and the gorgeous, melancholic 'Angel', Harry was alone in Digbeth once again as Boycie, Doug and Sam left the stage for him to perform accompanied only by his guitar.

'Gen Strange' was first, Harry forgetting the words to the second verse until prompted by the crowd, followed by the anthemic 'Kindness …' then the solo interlude closed with a lusty community singalong of 'Float Forever'. The rest of the band returned for the tune we'd been praying for above all others, one that they only perform as a special treat at sold-out shows.

'1998', from their first EP *Delicious*, is a truly epic transcendental soundscape and one of the finest pieces of rock music I've ever heard. Ten minutes later, the crowd is in a state of utter delirium. It would be a fitting way to close any show, but Peace have more than enough crowd-pleasers in their locker, and there were plenty to come. After calming things down with 'Scumbag' from the *In Love* album, Harry reminisced about his time spent 'walking these streets, wearing an advertising board for the Rainbow', by way of an introduction to the beautiful lament to Digbeth that is 'California Daze'.

'Drain' and the Afrobeat undertones of 'Bloodshake' fired up the mosh-pit mayhem once more, and yet again we were brought back down to earth with an emotional rendition of 'From Under Liquid Glass', which gradually builds towards an almighty crescendo of crashing drums and guitars. Next up was 'Wraith', a song about falling in love with a sex worker that, given the band spent much of their late teens in the vicinity of an infamous Digbeth knocking shop, might be a little bit autobiographical. It's also got the best singalong chorus of the set, and the crowd didn't disappoint. 'World Pleasure' gave Harry's brother Sam a chance to shine with a fantastically funky bass solo, and proceedings were brought to an end, after two pulsating hours, with an extended, joyously received 'Lovesick'.

The Birmingham indie scene is incredibly vibrant at the moment, and Peace are the Godfathers of it – the Original Gangsters. They set an incredibly high bar and a fine example for the likes of Sugarthief, Karkosa, Violet, Spilt Milk Society, The Clause and The Novus to follow (baby). They've all made a promising start, but if any of them live up to Peace's standards, Brum's gig-goers are in for a treat. It was a truly amazing concert by a band who are completely versed in the dynamics and emotional power of great rock music and deliver it with panache. I rank them alongside the best live guitar bands I've seen – The Jam and The Clash – and I emerged into the cold Digbeth night promising myself that I'll never miss them play in Birmingham again until one of us dies.

THE ETERNAL BATTLE FOR 'ME TIME'

LEKKY AND FRIENDS @ ACAPELLA, THE JEWELLERY QUARTER

We have a diary in our house in which me and my missus enter our plans, so they don't clash. It was my wife's idea – whoever gets in first, wins, no arguments. And if you believe that, I've got some magic beans for sale.

'I'm at the hairdressers Wednesday night at 7.30,' she said, all matter of fact.

'You might wanna check the diary,' I countered. 'I'm out that night.'

'Sod the diary,' she said, except she didn't say 'sod'. 'It's Valentine's Day the next day, then my birthday. I'm going to the hairdressers.'

Negotiations over. She wears the trousers in our house. I just iron them.

But as it turned out, she went straight from work and they saw her early. I rang to find out what time she'd be home, and she asked if I was missing her. Hmmm … this was awkward. She's hotter than the spoons in *Trainspotting*, of course I miss her.

'Erm, yeah,' I said. 'But I was thinking I might be able to make it to the gig.'

I'd annoyed her again, but by seven o'clock I was on the bus.

It's not easy raising a crew to go up town on a Wednesday night, especially when it's at such short notice and equidistant between paydays. But listening to The Clause on my phone while heading into the city gave me an idea, and I texted battle rapper Penance, who lives in Digbeth and has been a bit of a hermit lately, with the last thing I'd heard:

Locked in in the winter rain,
Afraid to show your face so you shy away,
Chin up son, wipe your tears away,
Where are you now?

My hotline soon blinged.

'On the 7.31 into New Street,' said the text.

'Cool. Meet me where Enoch Powell made his Rivers of Blood speech.'

'I'll be there for eight,' he replied.

That's the great thing about knocking around with people you've bored half to death with Birmingham cultural and historical references. He knew exactly where I meant, and I knew I need say nothing more, just get myself down to the Midland Hotel in Stephenson Street.

From there, we got the tram to St Paul's Square. It's only a pound/euro – they're equivalent now, aren't they? – but if you sit at the front, you've got a chance of disembarking before the conductor reaches you. Quite a few had the same idea, so there were no seats in the prime fare-dodging positions, but we still made it with our coin intact. I don't condone this type of behaviour, but battle rappers are a notoriously bad influence on me, and I'm always happy to inject a bit of drama into a review.

We walked up Ludgate Hill (site of the last public hanging in Birmingham – I hope it wasn't for fare dodging) and on to Frederick Street, and by twenty to nine I was saying hello to Lekky outside the joint. I've long been a fan of her melodic indie-rap and was chuffed to bits to speak to her.

'Have you been on?' I asked, a bit perturbed.

'Yeah, you missed me.'

Missing people was becoming a theme. Luckily, she was winding me up and I'd made it in plenty of time. Legend has it that Billy Page wrote the seminal mod classic 'The 'In' Crowd' for Dobie Gray after arriving in San Francisco one night and asking a taxi driver to take him to a cool hangout. The cabbie allegedly informed him that the 'in' crowd were at the Fillmore Theatre watching Aretha Franklin. This can't be true, as the song was written in 1964, when the Queen of Soul was still crooning jazz standards for Columbia Records, and wouldn't have attracted the kind of crowd that would fill the Fillmore. But it's a cool yarn and I lived a microcosm of it on Wednesday at the jam-packed Acapella bar in the Jewellery Quarter's Frederick Street, where a veritable who's who of Birmingham's urban music 'in' crowd was in attendance.

Multi-talented writer, singer and all-round socio-cultural authority AffieJam was standing at the bar as I walked in, while brilliant lyricist and rapper Truemendous, back home from London for a few days, was near the stage. Former Lady Sanity producer and Phan Tom Studios owner Adam Nightingale was there with his entourage, and soul singer Janel Antoneshia arrived just after me. Despite mingling with the glitterati, I was not too starstruck to enjoy the haunting melodies of Naomi Dawes, and rapper S Maverick also grabbed my attention with a gritty, energetic and entertaining performance.

Melody warrior Lekky was the one who I'd risked domestic strife to see, and she didn't disappoint. The Leamington-born assimilated Brummie opened with the cool, calm vibes of new single 'Tippy Toe', which has been on repeat in our house since it dropped a few days ago, and played live, the full-fat-funk of the band soon had the crowd getting into the groove along with them. New song 'Flicker' was next – a first listen for me, but the beat was infectious and I'm eagerly looking forward to being able to play it at home.

The short, sweet set closed with the gorgeous, mellow vibes of 'Meditate', a song that does exactly what it says on the tin with its trippy, trance-like chorus, the 'breathe in, breathe out' mantra verging on therapeutic. Top of the bill was Gambimi, who entertained us with some smooth and sexy RnB. There followed a series of minute-long open-mic spots that only went to show the amazing depth of talent with which Birmingham is blessed. Even so, it was great to see the more established stars, Janel Antoneshia and AffieJam get up for a laugh, in the process saving the venue some coin on cleaning as they wiped the floor with everybody.

Acapella is a smart new venue, a real asset to JQ nightlife with a relaxed and friendly door policy, and it was a great night put on by I Luv Live and the venue owner, Seamus. 'You don't sound Irish,' I said to him, confused by his Middle Eastern-sounding accent.

'No, it's the Turkish version of Seamus,' he replied with a smile. He'll fit right in in Brum.

Penance and I walked back into town via Ludgate Hill, and the history of the place, combined with the wet weather, reminded me of a story Our Dad told me about his mate who was a warden at HMP Winson Green. One day, he had to escort a prisoner to the gallows, where he was to be hanged for murder, and as they crossed the yard the heavens opened.

'Bloody hell,' said the condemned man. 'As if today wasn't bad enough.'

'How do you think I feel?' replied Dad's mate, 'I've gorra walk back in it.'

IN THE CITY

After reading this, the band paid me the ultimate compliment by naming their debut EP *Rock and Road* and their second one *Rock and Road Part II*.

CITYLIGHTZ @ O2 ACADEMY

Wolverhampton band CityLightz first came to my attention – or more accurately grabbed me by the lapels and screamed down my ear – via their song 'Tim', a story of upsetting the wrong guy and regretting it when your mates tell you he's a right nutter and he's gunning for you. Been there, done that, had the stitches.

I found it profoundly evocative as I had an old workmate of the same name – employed at our place specifically on the strength of his violent temper. The gaffer was hoping there'd be a clash of personalities with a particularly troublesome shop steward, but they ended up best mates, so management's cunning plan failed miserably, as do most of their cunning plans.

Tim's reputation preceded him. He was a colleague's father-in-law and I'd already heard many tales of madness straight from the son-in-law's mouth, including one gruesome encounter involving a police raid, an Alsatian and a kitchen knife, which ended in the dog's death and a successful self-defence plea. Probably the hardest thing to reconcile was the rep and the name. I mean, it's short for Timothy for God's sake. It's hardly Chopper or Slasher, is it?

Anyway, you really have to hear the song to know how it resonated with me, and it led to the band and I exchanging a few tweets, and me blagging myself onto the guest list. Son number one met me in Subside to borrow a few quid but told me he couldn't afford to come to the show, while ordering two double JD and cokes. 'No wonder you can't afford it,' I said, as I puffed on a wafer-thin roll-up made of smuggled tobacco, and occasionally sipped my half of mild. I can ALWAYS afford it.

CITYLIGHTZ. (© MATT CROCKFORD PHOTOGRAPHY)

Son number two landed and it was time to head for the Academy, via a back-street shortcut that brought us out directly opposite the venue but the wrong side of eight lanes of traffic, a couple of impenetrable steel fences and a cavernous road tunnel. Should have gone the long way.

Two of the band were outside, and a couple of nicer, more grounded blokes you'd struggle to meet, and after telling them about my mate Tim, we went in to catch the support. I only caught the last bit of Kidderminster's Shiraz Hempstock – born in Israel, where her name means 'secret song', as her mom explained to me. Thanks Sarah, and sorry for assuming you named your daughter after your favourite tipple.

Shiraz finished her set with an ambitious and impressive version of 'The Chain' by Fleetwood Mac, a band I've been a fan of for at least six months, ever since discovering that bona fide song-writing genius Christine McVie is from Bear-wood. Next on the bill were Methods, who warmed things up nicely with their moody Editors vibe. I was impressed enough to grab a CD of their *Fires* EP and I'm pretty sure I will enjoy investigating further.

CityLightz opened their set with recently released single 'Proof', blessed with all the usual energy and uncompromising lyrics. Singer/guitarist Luke and lead vocalist/rapper B give off a Dave Wakeling/Ranking Roger vibe, and The Beat aren't the only band I'm reminded of as the Wolverhampton five-piece tear through their set-list. I'm thinking Black Country Beastie Boys one minute, Yam-Yams With Attitude the next.

B is a real character on the mic, and he leads the crowd through a jokey sing-along on 'Had Enough'. But don't let that blind you to his serious MC skills. His grimy bars are interspersed with killer hooks passionately sung by Luke. Close your eyes and it could be Slash on lead guitar, rather than unassuming, down-to-earth Adam. All this as bassist James and drummer Tom provide a driving beat while simultaneously looking like they're trying to murder their instruments.

A rhythmic guitar riff, overlaid by another one reminiscent of Nolan Porter's 'If I Could only be Sure', builds to a crescendo on the band's debut single 'Don't Know Me', before the verses start and remind you of the Arctic Monkeys, but with better accents. This is followed by 'Where I'm From', in which the band refuse to be judged by their working-class roots. I'm from Chelmsley Wood lads – I don't look down on anybody.

'Elevator' is next, its powerful chorus delivered at breakneck speed. The band then aim their sights at the police and their informers on 'Piggy', before closing the show with the aforementioned story of the bad boy from a broken home, 'Tim'. I left with a smile on my face and one of Tom's discarded drumsticks in my pocket.

CityLightz are going places. They've only been together a matter of months and have already been shortlisted for BBC WM's 'Sound of 2019' and are nominated for a prize or two at the Birmingham Music Awards in May. They're an incredibly exciting and accomplished live band, musically dynamic and powerful, their lyrics funny and thought provoking. All five of them look like they're having as much fun as their audience, and each member makes a massive, vital contribution . They combine Road-man bars with a complete mastery of classic rock and, in doing so, have given birth to what I believe is a new genre. I know, it's only Rock 'n' Road, but I like it.

PROMOTION CLAUSE

There's a new flame in town …

THE CLAUSE @ DIGBETH INSTITUTE 2

I got the bad news that this gig had sold out from the world's premier rock and road band CityLightz at their Academy show in January. I was crestfallen as The Clause are one of my favourite groups and I'd been looking forward to it, but the fact that an unsigned act with no label, management or national radio play had sold out such a big show had taken me by surprise. All was not lost, however – the band and I follow each other on Twitter and, hoping that they'd held a few tickets back, I slid into their DMs with a cheeky request.

Me: Any tickets left lads?

The Clause: Yeah, what's your address?

Me: **, ***** ****, Chelmsley Wood, Birmingham. (No one from the Wood adds Solihull to their address – we're proud Brummies, and to hell with property values and cheaper home insurance).

The Clause: I live in Kingshurst fella, opposite Lady Leshurr. Wanna meet me outside Asda at midday tomorrow?

Sorted.

After a couple of pre-gig pints at the Victoria (my favourite city-centre boozer now I'm boycotting Wetherspoons), I become part of a boisterous crowd waiting for four moddy-looking young geezers from Birmingham to play the Digbeth Institute. It's a walk down memory lane for me, as my own gang of four moddy-looking young geezers from Birmingham played the same venue thirty years previous. Our manifesto was to walk like the Kray twins and sing like The Jam – we had the walk off to a tee, but I suspect we probably sang like the Krays as well.

I wasn't the only one looking forward to seeing the band. Among those in attendance I spotted the force of nature that is Genie Mendez from electro-pop trio Lycio; Jack Sanders, the actor who plays me so well stumbling down Lower

Trinity Street in The Clause's Tokyo video; Mark Piddington, who was filming the gig for the best music show on the internet, *Raw Sound TV*; and the indefatigable AffieJam, who told me she is contemplating doing a cover of 'Tainted Love' – I put her straight on the lyrics that all other covers of Gloria Jones' Northern Soul monument have got wrong and got on with looking forward to the brilliant reimagining of the song that she'll no doubt come up with.

Unprofessional as ever, I missed the first three support acts, Here Casino, La Dharma and Glass Ceilings, but I already know that La Dharma are good (check out their sumptuous indie masterpiece 'Sirens'), and at least saw KANVAS fire up the mosh pit with a great version of 'I Bet You Look Good on the Dancefloor', before the headliners took the stage to a heroes' welcome on the latest leg of their sold-out nationwide tour.

Lead guitarist (and Asda-based ticket distributor) Liam Deakin kicked things off with the hypnotic riff of fourth single 'Tokyo', a song so undeniably great they must be tempted to open with it, close with it and throw it in as an encore. Luckily, they don't need to, as they can follow it up with third single 'Sixteen', a song so undeniably great they must be tempted to open with it, close with it and … you get the picture.

Frontman Pearce Macca, 6ft of pure charisma in an ice-blue suit, is just as elegant lyrically as he is sartorially. 'I'm in awe/as your lips wrap round the straw/ of a strawberry daiquiri', he sings, and though I'm sure The Clause are rock and roll enough to know that you don't drink strawberry daiquiri through a straw, you also don't discard a line that good just to mollify pedants like me. It's my favourite Brummie lyric since Lady Leshurr said, 'My bars touch the kids like R Kelly' in 'Queen's Speech 7'.

A quartet of new songs followed – 'Cigarette Kiss', 'Hate the Player', 'Comedown Conversations' and 'Vive La Revolucion' – but it was a quartet of Jägerbombs for a tenner at the bar and I was having too good a time to make notes on individual songs. The overall vibe though, was unforgettable, whatever you were drinking (Rohypnol aside).

Bassist Jonny Fyffe has the same no-nonsense, detached air of The Who's John Entwistle, while drummer Niall Fennell is such a Reni-from-the-Stone Roses-level genius on the kit that I'm tempted to forgive the beard. Almost. In my opinion facial hair is one of those things, like three-quarter-length trackie bottoms, that only look good on a black man.

The rhythm section laid a solid foundation for the guitar pyrotechnics of Liam and Pearce, and together the boys are greater than the sum of their parts. It seems they all bring different influences to bear – the look and feel of sixties mod and nineties Britpop are obvious, but there is more to it than that. One minute I was reminded of Maroon 5, next it was the Scissor Sisters, while echoes of The Killers were never far away.

We got back on familiar punky-indie territory with second single 'Golden Age', then violinist Lukas Evans joined the lads to add lashings of melancholy to the song that proves the band are already at that magical point where crowds are singing their songs back to them. It's the best ballad Noel Gallagher never wrote, and it'll sound brilliant when they play it at Glastonbury. (Yeah, I said it.) An achingly beautiful lament, it could be about a relative who has passed away, a friend you've fallen out with, an ex-partner, or maybe all three. It's called 'Where are you Now?' and personally I was singing it to the deaf and blind record label A & R people who've failed to sign this brilliant band.

Another new song, 'In my Element', was a worthy prelude to the big finish, their first single 'Shut me Out'. A fitting finale for me, as I spent the rest of the night up the road at the always enjoyable Northern Soul night at the Big Bull's Head, before getting home in the small hours to find that my lovely-but-fed-up wife had shut me out, to ensure she had the chance to tear a strip off me when I got back. Ah well, no hardship – she's even more beautiful when she's angry.

Anyway, as I was saying, The Clause are going to be a huge success, and I've never been so sure of anything since I first heard this year's Brit Awards winner, Walsall's finest Jorja Smith.

But enough of all that, I hear you cry, you want to know whatever happened to MY band, don't you? Sadly, it all ended in tears and ignominy after a New Year's Eve gig at an Irish pub, where we were booked by a panicked landlord when his preferred option of a more traditional band cancelled at the last minute. Not surprisingly, we were free, and ready, willing and able to help out, but halfway through our reggae version of The Temptations' 'Just my Imagination', some-one from the crowd shouted, 'Can't you do something Irish?' Unfortunately, our (Irish) drummer responded with, 'We can go outside and dig up the car park if you like!' and we just about escaped with our limbs and instruments intact. Our 'career', on the other hand, lay in ruins. It was a mercy killing. We were hopeless. A totally different trajectory awaits The Clause – remember, I told you.

DIGBETH CALLING

Have you heard about those police stings in America set up to catch wanted fugitives, where they fool the miscreants into thinking they've won some incredible prize then arrest them when they show up to collect it? Well, here's a heads up for West Midlands' finest – if ever you want me, just put a time and place on a poster, write 'AffieJam' on it, and in the words of the Jackson Five, I'll be there.

That's why, having got up for work at four that morning, and faced with the prospect of doing the same thing the next, I put on my long johns, buttoned up my coat against the bitter cold and headed for Digbeth on a damned Thursday …

HOUSE OF VIBES – A SORT OF OPEN-MIC NIGHT AT THE NIGHT OWL, STARRING AFFIEJAM, MADI SASKIA, KOFI STONE AND TEHILLAH HENRY

The event was called House of Vibes, organised by Soultribe, and was on at my favourite club, the Night Owl. Normally, I'm there on non-school nights until the early hours listening to Northern Soul and sixties RnB spun by their fantastic DJs, Paul Cook and Mazzy Snape, but tonight was an altogether different proposition – a live showcase for some of Birmingham's best emerging talent. It was more structured than an open-mic night, but still a fairly loose arrangement, with the artists coming and going to help with each other's backing vocals and the like.

First up was Chrissie A, accompanied by guitarist Tom, who did a promising number of her own and a nice cover of Michael Jackson's 'Rock With You'. She was followed by Rochae, backed on guitar by tonight's headliner, AffieJam. Rochae can often be seen and heard playing tom-toms for Namywa, but tonight she treated us to some developing ideas of her own. Big potential was hinted at when she sang her excellent debut 'Driving', which had the packed house singing along to an infectious chorus.

Next up was local rapper Kofi Stone, who got the place jumping with some dope hip-hop. He performed his own jams 'Nothin' ain't Free', 'Stories in Pyjamas' and

AFFIE JAM. (©LIBI PEDDER)

'Message to Her' – all available on the net and well worth checking out. On arrival, I'd seen Madi Saskia in the beer garden/blazing area and hoped she was performing. I'm delighted to report that my wish came true.

She opened with her own song 'Dreamin'', accompanied brilliantly by Tehillah Henry on guitar and the multi-talented Rochae beating out a driving rhythm on somebody's mic'd-up guitar case. She then absolutely slayed it with a cover of Mahalia's 'Sober'. Now, I love Mahalia, but Madi's impassioned delivery left me a little bit emotionally drained and feeling like I'd heard the song properly for the first time. Dripping with painful personal experience, it was what I imagine an actual human heart breaking would sound like. Madi is every inch the Soul Diva on stage but refreshingly modest and humble off it. She's rubbish at taking compliments, but on tonight's performance she's going to have to get used to it.

She then left the stage free for talented singer-songwriter Tehillah to perform a couple of her own soul-tinged folky originals and a wonderfully reimagined version of 'I will Survive'. Rapper Jay Grant came on to whip the crowd up some more with his quickfire grimy bars, joined at one point by Rochae, who delivered a ridiculously catchy hook on one of the songs.

The crowd was so hyped by now that I was beginning to wonder how Affie-Jam's gentler sound would follow this madness. From reading her well-written and enlightening blogs, I know she's not blessed with the supreme confidence her talent warrants and if I, as a huge fan, was worried, then I thought she might be too. But while, in real life, she may have insecurities, to the casual observer she possesses an ungodly amount of sass.

Someone once told her she was too cool to be from Birmingham. This clown had obviously never seen Steel Pulse singing 'Ku Klux Klan' on the BBC wearing appropriate headgear, or the Peaky Blinders walking in slow motion, or a 15-year-old Steve Winwood possessed by the spirit of Ray Charles, or 'Pass the Dutchie' being the first black video ever played on MTV, or the dancers at the Night Owl. But Affie's reply was great – 'I'm cool BECAUSE I'm from Birmingham.'

She came onstage boosted by winning a CD in an impromptu quiz (FIX!) and looking as effortlessly stylish as ever in baseball cap, glorious blonde braids, skinny jeans and Doctor Marten boots. She kicked off with the achingly beautiful 'Put Aside' and from the opening bars she and backing vocalist Jabez Walsh had the crowd eating out of the palms of their hands. The chemistry between the two of them is really something – I'd like to see him performing with her every time and not just when she's nervous, as she says is the case tonight.

Affie's total command of the room is emphasised on her lovely cover of Little Dragon's 'Twice', when the sound drops to nothing but her voice and finger snaps. As the crowd join in, it's as if she's put a spell on us. The two-part harmonies that grace the next song, 'Babel', are something Fleet Foxes would be proud of – so intricate, polished and layered you're checking to see if there are still only two of them on stage.

Affie closes her short-but-oh-so-sweet set with an imaginative and emotionally charged cover of 'Smells Like Teen Spirit'. I join in the calls for an encore but feel like a fraud as I have to sprint off into the night hoping to get three or four hours' kip before my horrendously early start in the morning.

On the journey home, I reflect on the fact that I've seen her live four times now and still not seen her perform my two favourite songs (which she's too cool to bother thinking up proper titles for). My consolation is that I always enjoy seeing her so much I hardly notice at the time. That's how cool she is.

DON'T STOP THIEF

A controversial one at the time, now stripped of unintentional offence and with The Cosmics reinstated. Sorry Erin, I hope you like this one better …

SUGARTHIEF, SPILT MILK SOCIETY, THE COSMICS @ 02 DIGBETH INSTITUTE 3

It's not easy you know, this reviewing lark. Contrary to what my wife thinks, I don't just hang around Digbeth all the time, smoking, drinking and waiting for great local artists to put on gigs. Not ALL the time. Sometimes I go to King's Heath.

But seriously, it's more complicated than that – a job, two young kids and a grown-up family of battle rappers take up a lot of time. For instance, my son Tydal has got a gig next Saturday, so that's a must-see, and the indie scene in Brum is so crowded it's increasingly difficult to keep up.

All this means I have to apply ruthless quality control to the dozens of gigs taking place each month. This particular show, to launch Sugarthief's debut EP, was crossed off my list due to other commitments, but kept making eyes at me on social media, and every time I heard the new collection's opening track 'Good Luck, I Hope You Make It' on the radio, it was like they were trying to hypnotise me into coming.

I thought I had plenty of time to make up my mind, then heard there were only sixty tickets left. I finally decided to cancel everything else and go, only to find I'd lost my credit card and the 'sold out' signs had gone up. After a brief moment of sweet despair, I resorted to begging emails to the band, starting with 'I don't usually do this', moving through 'I interviewed UB40 the other day' and ending up at 'Somebody on Twitter said I was Brum's finest music writer'. (I didn't really say that, but sod it, I have now.) It eventually worked, and I even managed to get a plus two on the guest list for my mates, the music-biz power couple behind the Birmingham Music Awards, Jo Jeffries and Simon Pitt, although one of them was going to have to pretend to be a photographer.

It's a stellar line-up – a Who's Who of BMA nominees – three of the greatest Great White Hopes from the burgeoning Birmingham scene. They've all been supported by the likes of BBC *Introducing*, and Steve Lamacq, Huw Stephens and others on Radio One, yet still occupy that sweet spot where you can see them at intimate venues, playing to a few hundred wild, young, adoring fans.

We walked in halfway through The Cosmics playing the gorgeous 'Trust is Blind' – my only criticism being that the dreamy opening doesn't go on for longer before crashing into a maelstrom of feedback and distortion. In fact, there'd be no complaints from me if the dreamy opening went on forever.

We settled down at the back for some no-nonsense garage-punk, delivered at 100 miles an hour, with 50,000 watts of power, like The Ramones fronted by Debbie Harry. Lead singer Erin Grace oozes charisma and attitude and has a voice not the slightest bit lost in the high volume generated by the band. There are slight problems with the sound, but Erin and her cousins Danny and Conor blow them away with a wall of sound that makes it difficult to believe there are only three of them. They power through their biggest tune, 'Johnny', and follow this up with two new songs, 'Brainfuzz' and 'Eyes', before crowd favourite 'Cundy Get Down' closes the show in suitably chaotic style. Anarchy in the O2.

Next up are the slightly more subtle sounds of Spilt Milk Society, Harry Handford returning to his main job after moonlighting as producer of the headliners' new EP. The strength of his band lies in the song writing, all lovely melodies and catchy hooks that prove that Harry has truly mastered the craft. I think it's fair to say that the B-Town bands of the early 2010s sowed the seeds of the new Madlands movement and though 'Spilly' Milk have moved to Liverpool for uni, their amalgam of elements of Peace and Swim Deep could only have been forged here in the King City. This is especially true of 'She Tastes Like Summer', a beautiful tune that has been shamelessly stolen for an ad campaign by a big Spanish telecoms company who haven't paid them a penny in royalties. Still, it's helped the band to over 3 million Spotify streams, so it's not all doom and gloom. They finish their set by showing their versatility and out-punking even The Cosmics with a storming version of 'Cops and Robbers'.

Sugarthief are another band who offer a nod towards B-Town prime movers Peace – all Converse, choruses and curtain hairdos – and like Peace, they have the brothers thing going on with frontman Jordi and guitarist Jack. Their star has been on the rise since The Twang saw them at the Beyond the Tracks festival and invited them onto their last two winter tours. They were named best indie band at last year's BMAs and are in the running again for the overall title this year alongside the likes of UB40, The Specials and Ocean Colour Scene.

The headliners open with the aforementioned 'Good Luck', followed by the brilliant 'Modern Man', both off the new *I Before E*(P), the title a hint to people who have trouble spelling their name, and the new collection is played in its seven-song entirety throughout the set. A cover of 'Dancing in the Moonlight', with Tim Senna on tambourine, is thrown in alongside crowd favourites 'Provide', 'When Did It All Go So Wrong?', and the best thing to come out of Birmingham since Jack Grealish, 'Joy Affair', accompanied by a stealthy bit of crowd surfing by Jordi. They planned to finish with 'Things I Heard' from the new EP, but were forced into that rare thing, an impromptu encore, by the crowd relentlessly singing the bass-line introduction to 'When Did It All Go So Wrong?' until they simply HAD to play it again.

A great night, and while the youngsters headed for Snobs to carry on partying, the more sophisticated among us retire to Café Collette in Lower Trinity Street to warm down and reflect on the ever-growing Madlands magic weaving its way around the second city.

SUGARTHIEF. (© LEE CRAWFORD, DISTORTED IMAGE PHOTOGRAPHY)

LOVE MUSIC, HATE RACISM

The title says it all, it could be my epitaph …

KIOKO, NAMYWA AND OTHERS @ THE CROSSING, DIGBETH

I love music, and I really, REALLY hate racism, so when I clocked this event on Twitter the other week, I thought it might be right up my street. Love Music Hate Racism is a fledgling movement, run along similar lines to its predecessor Rock Against Racism (RAR), which peaked in the late seventies when Steel Pulse and The Clash played to 80,000 people under the RAR banner at Victoria Park in London. As the far right rears its ugly head again, a grassroots anti-racism movement is something I'm more than happy to support. Call me a snowflake if you like, but what do a lot of snowflakes make? An avalanche.

I arranged to meet my posse, which included my old mate Pete Rogers, in the Big Bull's Head in Digbeth High Street, where our mate Sainy was on the decks. Pete is the spitting image of my idol Paul Weller, and also does a wicked John Weller impression by managing his son, Sam, the talented singer-songwriter and frontman of White Flag Dares. Somewhat ironically, on a night like that one, it was in that boozer where I suffered a bit of nationalist prejudice many moons ago, when my good friend, the late, great Garry Twist and I were asked by an angry bigot what we were doing in an Irish pub. Now Garry was a very laid-back kind of chap, good-humoured and the kindest man you could ever wish to meet, but he was no shrinking violet and not easily intimidated. He advised the Irishman in rather less polite terms than I'm using here that were he to get a shovel and dig a hole in the floor he would find Brummagem, not Ireland, and that we'd drink wherever we like in this city, thanks very much.

Times must have changed in the intervening years because, on this occasion, the only time I got picked on for my ethnicity was when a couple of Welsh tourists got me and my mate to say, 'By order of the Peaky Blinders' while they filmed us on their phones. As warm and welcoming as the Bull's Head was, with

DJ Sainy cooking up a storm on the decks, the TV was showing some terrible repeat called 'Man Utd are on telly again' so we headed for the gig, handily located about 30 yards down the road.

The Crossing is one of Digbeth's hidden gems, a 600-capacity venue within the confines of South and City College on the High Street. There was a good crowd in there, including luminaries of the local music scene like AffieJam and Lady Sanity, and numbers were further boosted by some old comrades from a political party that I used to be a member of in my radical younger days (I'll give you a clue which one in a minute).

Local rapper Kurly got the (Socialist Workers) Party started and he was followed by Wolverhampton's Vital, joined on one track by B-Nice. Zara Sykes got a great reaction from the crowd and Kofi Stone, having impressed at the Night Owl last month, was again in sparkling form. The performances were interspersed with impressive speeches from the likes of Eleanor Smith, the new black MP for Enoch Powell's former constituency (BOOM!) and a deeply moving call for justice from Kadisha Brown-Burrell, sister of Kingsley Burrell, who was killed in police custody after calling them himself for help.

Top of the bill were Kioko, a multi-racial reggae band who come with a copper-bottomed guarantee of Good Times, which is also the title of one of their songs. Highlights of their set include the wistful 'Let's Be Frank', a great version of Drake's 'Hotline Bling' and show closer 'Deadly Roots', all of which went down a storm. Oh, and 'Queen of the Dancefloor' – just, WOW! Their best yet. I challenge anyone to go and see them and leave without a smile on your face.

Kioko are a great band, and we're lucky to catch them on a night off from their seemingly eternal world tour supporting UB40, but for me the show was stolen by the act that preceded them, the incredible Namywa and her brilliant band. Even though they were limited by time constraints to four numbers, quality counts, and her tunes certainly have an abundance of that. It's no exaggeration for me to say that hers would account for about half of my favourite dozen songs released over the last two years and, played live, they go to another level.

She opens with a breathless version of 'Wound Up', built on the funky riffing of guitarist Ben Jones and embellished magnificently by Madi Saskia on backing vocals. This is followed with two new songs, 'Everything You Do' and 'Matter of Fact', and that she performs unreleased tracks in such a big show says everything about the belief she must have in them. Such confidence is justified – I was completely blown away by the new stuff.

In between songs Namywa tries to list the genres touched upon in her music, but to do it justice she'd be talking all night. Her sound incorporates many aspects of black music – reggae, neo-soul, funk, RnB, gospel – you name it, it's in

there somewhere. She gives it the all-encompassing title of 'Afrotwang', which I suppose is as good a word as any, but that's just the musical styles. When you move on to the lyrics and general mood of the songs you need a whole new set of adjectives – melancholic, joyous, celebratory, profound, to name but a few; militant, poetic, heart-breaking, defiant, to name a few more. Live with her full band, powered by a hench rhythm section and Rochae deadly as ever on the bongos as well as contributing vocals, Namywa is quite simply a force of nature.

Seemingly possessed by the music, at one point a ponytail about as long as she is almost decapitates Madi as it whirls around behind her. She closes the set with 'Jungle', which morphs into 'Girls Just Wanna Have Fun' and Madi singing 'Mo' Money Mo' Problems' without missing a beat. I felt deflated when they left the stage quicker than I anticipated but apparently there's a headline show coming up, so I'll just have to console myself with that. In the meantime I'm hoping nearly as hard as she is for one track to go viral, or one appearance on something like Jools Holland, which I'm convinced would be the making of her and give her the audience she deserves. As I left, I worried about writing a review because I couldn't think past one word – phenomenal.

To complete the story of the night, I was waiting for the last No. 97 on Digbeth High Street when a girl approached me and asked very politely for a cigarette. I obliged, and she said, 'Do you want business?' I graciously declined and feeling sorry for her, gave her the rest of my fags, hoping she might be tempted to just go home and have a cup of tea and a smoke. She walked off and I watched as she leaned into a few car windows – she didn't seem to get any takers, bless her. Then a beggar came up to me and asked if I had 80p, so he could get chicken and chips. Sadly, all I had was my daysaver bus ticket. '80p for chicken & chips!' I said. 'Have you got 80p for me fam?'

I love Digbeth. It's such an adventure if you know where to look.

JUDGING JEFFRIES

An impromptu trip into town results in a happy coincidental meeting with one of the driving forces of the Birmingham music scene ...

Having taken the kids to school and with no work until the afternoon, I was taking a leisurely walk home with my favourite tunes in my headphones. Today it was The Jam caressing my ears (just for a change), and their unofficial national anthem 'That's Entertainment' inspired me to do something constructive with my weekday. Days of speed and slow-time Mondays had been and gone, and now it was pissing down with rain on a boring Wednesday, but when you're an old boy about town with some free time and a new Jasper Conran raincoat to rock, it doesn't have to be that way.

I fancied a stroll round town, there was a 97 bus going my way, and I decided to catch it and see what was going on in the city. I shared the journey with my old mate David George, author of Birmingham City hoolie-book *Apex To Zulu*, who was on his way to give a talk on the futility and horror of knife crime and gang violence to some youngsters. Poacher turned gamekeeper perhaps, but his experience and credibility on the subject can sometimes be just what's needed to gain the respect and attention of the hardest – and hardest to reach – kids.

Two published authors from Chelmsley Wood on the same bus – what are the odds? We went our separate ways on arrival in town, and with the rain still falling and 0121 my oyster, I opted for the fine fare and free Wi-Fi of Café Artum, a creative hotspot that I'd been meaning to visit since it opened last year.

Selling an unusual mix of coffee, tea, art, vegan cakes and vinyl records, this cool independent venture is located in the buff-terracotta Coleridge Chambers, one of Brum's most beautiful buildings, yet it hardly even stands out, for amongst its neighbours are the magnificent Methodist Central Hall and the equally stunning Victoria Law Courts.

I imagine this area has barely changed since Conan-Doyle wrote about it in one of his Sherlock Holmes adventures. Even the steps outside are a work of art, and standing on them waiting for opening time, I was delighted to see the small frame and big personality of Jo Jeffries and her able assistant, social media whizz-kid Lucy Ballard. We went inside and I got the teas in, because if you know Jo, you'll also know that the last thing this blonde ball of energy needs is too much caffeine, even if it is locally sourced from the wonderful Quarter Horse Coffee Roasters in Bristol Street.

I lit the blue touchpaper by asking about the Birmingham Music Awards that she co-founded, and Jo went off like a Catherine wheel.

It's hectic. I'm in constant contact with artists, finding out who's coming, who's performing, etc. Some are contemplating flying back from touring to be here. We had a great night at the Glee Club last year, but we couldn't go again this year – we needed more capacity. This time we've got 750 coming to The Mill, at the old Rainbow Venues in Lower Trinity Street. There are 36 categories of awards and loads of live performances. It's a lot to fit in between 6 and 10.30, but there's always the after-party! Could be an all-nighter! The standard tickets are £25 and the VIP section, where you're in your own booth with waitress service and champagne, is £85. There are also sponsor packages where you get to present an award and are given prominent positioning and exposure for your business or organisation.

Any big names among the nominations?

Loads. UB40, the Specials, Lady Leshurr, Mist, Jaykae, the Streets, Peace, Dapz On The Map, who's just signed to Sony. And Jorja Smith, who just won Best Female at the Brit Awards. The indie/alternative category is mad – Sugarthief, Ivory Wave, The Clause and Karkosa are all nominated, and the MCs and RnB categories are incredibly strong – Sanity, Vital, Safone, Lotto Boyz, Namywa, Call Me Unique, Sicnis, Yatez, Stardom, Mayday – so many strong contenders. There are also some nice surprises that I can't reveal yet.

Who's gonna win?

Ha ha! Nobody knows! There's a public vote on the Rising Star category, and the rest of the voting is next Friday, when all the judges and ambassadors are meeting up at ACM music school's Birmingham Campus in the Jewellery Quarter, before going to UB40's album signing at HMV in the Bull Ring. It will all be voted on by local artists, DJs, music industry professionals, journalists, what have you. They'll be the ones to decide who wins, and they can vote in all the categories unless they're nominated in them. We can't have people voting for themselves!

BIRMINGHAM MUSIC AWARDS – JO JEFFRIES, JOHN TAYLOR, DEAN WILLIAMS, ACE. (© STEWART LAWLEY)

Fair enough. You co-founded the awards, what inspired you?

I want Birmingham to become recognised as a world music city. We've definitely got the talent, but we hide our light behind a bushel too much. We also lack infrastructure, we need to tempt record company A & R people to the city. The aim is to grow the awards and make it something that national and even global media want to cover. But it's also about giving recognition to the people working hard already to build the city's reputation, be they artists, promoters, websites, labels, producers, venues, DJs, blogs, all sorts. And to reflect the incredible depth and diversity of the talent of course.

What's in it for the performers?

The sky's the limit. Last year Kioko performed and did a UB40 cover in their set. A couple of the UB40 lads crashed the stage and after the show offered them the support slot on their thirty-date tour. Kioko ended up playing at the Royal Albert Hall and their following on social media exploded from hundreds to thousands. It changed their lives.

Breathe, Jo.

And put me down for a couple of tickets. I can't wait.

FIGURE IT OUT

LADY SANITY CELEBRATES THE RELEASE OF HER BRILLIANT FOR FIGURES EP WITH A LAUNCH PARTY IN DIGBETH

Organising my squad for this event was a logistical nightmare. I managed to book my last half-day of annual leave for a Friday evening – a rare concession involving a Faustian pact that required me to do a full day's work in half a shift. I really didn't want the gaffer to know I could do that – but needs must. I then had to overcome bad credit and even worse computer literacy to get e-tickets sent to my phone.

So, after all that, my instructions for everyone to meet in Subside at 7 p.m. seemed like the easy bit.

Not for my lot – I was the first one there and drinking alone for a while in what was supposed to be happy hour. Cousin Mark's train from London was delayed and my son Kurtis, still on his way home from work in Telford, was shocked to learn that the gig was tonight. 'I thought it was next Friday,' whined the chaotic overgrown teenager. By 7.30 two more of my kids, Kirsty and up-and-coming grime sensation Tydal, were still waiting for a taxi in Washwood Heath, while my mate Lee was waiting for a bus and freezing his bits off in Castle Brom.

I knew the feeling, stood outside the boozer with only a wizened old Hell's Angel doorman for company. This unholy alliance of mod and rocker were scanning Digbeth High Street for the latecomers, which was nice of him, if a bit futile, as he had no idea what any of my firm looked like.

First to arrive was Mark, who eagerly approached the bar to buy me a drink and pay me for his ticket, until it dawned on him, after searching his wallet about fifteen times, that all his money was in the work gear that his brother had taken home to Handsworth Wood. Next to land were three of my kids (plus one girlfriend) who, being out with their dad, didn't feel the need to bring any money. Now we were only waiting for my mate Lee, so I rang him:

'I'm here,' he said.

'I can't see you,' I replied.

'I'm up the bar watching the Villa game on telly. We're losing 1–0.'

'The football's not on in here.'

'Oh perish it!' he said (except he didn't say 'peri'). 'I'm at the Irish Centre aren't I?'

Five minutes later, mob deep at last, we headed towards the venue, down Allison Street and past Digbeth Police Station. I'd only been to Suki10c once before, and not from this direction, so as a couple of coppers came out the back door of the clink I asked if I was going the right way. One stared back menacingly as if I was asking for a knocking shop (try saying the name of the place fast), but luckily his more clued-up colleague gave us directions.

On to the show, and Sanity was joined by Madi Saskia who, as well as being an integral part of Namywa's great band, has produced some beautiful music of her own recently. Sure enough, she brought a whole heap of magic to opening number 'They Won't Hear A Word' and completely justified the equal billing suggested by the two mics front and centre. Sanity went solo on vocal duties for 'Stuck' and then on 'Just Us' we were blessed with the spellbinding vocals of Elle Chante, who went on to perform her own sensual and enchanting song 'The Midas Touch'. No Sanity gig would be complete without her melancholic tribute to Birmingham, 'Yellow', and this was followed by the low-fi hip-hop of 'Blueprint' and the diamond-hard bars of 'Future'.

Trademark Blud was next to share vocals with the headliner – his modus operandi is to GO IN (as I believe da kidz say) and he didn't disappoint as he brought fire to 'No Limits' and left the stage to enthusiastic cheers from the packed house.

We were then treated to a couple of tunes from Sanity's brilliant *Summer in September* mixtape, namely 'Bars for the Bin' and 'Kinda Funny'. It may have been a cold December night in Digbeth but songs from that collection always remind me of the New York heatwave that caused all the trouble in Spike Lee's *Do The Right Thing*.

I was having too much fun to take notes, so I can't recall the song in which Sanity played the old Soul Train trick of parting the crowd to allow solo dancers the freedom of the floor. I do remember our Kirsty taking advantage and tripping over an acrobatic break-dancer behind her – we shouted a warning, but she just thought we were chanting her name!

Local legend, Call Me Unique helped keep the temperature rising, joining Sanity for a storming cover of Erykah Badu's 'On and On', and for a few delicious moments I almost convinced myself I was at an intimate early Fugees gig. As the fantastic backing band left the stage, they were more than adequately replaced by the beat-boxing and guitar of Ed Geater, accompanying Sanity on a haunting version of 'Found a Place', their brilliant recent collaboration.

The final phase of the show was just Sanity and her DJ performing 'Dreaming', 'Role Models', 'Can't Say' and 'Go the Distance'. I've been listening to 'Role

Models' in the house for a couple of weeks now, thinking it might be her best tune yet, and seeing the crowd reaction confirmed my suspicions. It has more of a grime vibe than her previous stuff and it really suits her.

Show-closer 'Go The Distance' is also an absolute banger that had the place lit like a Christmas tree, and with that, Sanity left the stage to a thunderous ovation. My grown-up kids certainly enjoyed it more than my little ones, Amber and Lewis, did when I took them to a free daytime Sanity show at the Bull Ring a few months back when Amber cried because it was too loud.

When I suggested getting the last bus because I had run out of money, Kirsty suddenly remembered she had some and we headed to the Night Owl for the un-official after-party. Round every corner we passed huge crowds of people queue-ing up for places that looked more like drop forges than clubs, and I reflected on what a vibrant, quirky, talented city we're lucky enough to live in.

We finally left the Owl at about 3 a.m. with Call Me Unique still throwing shapes on the dance floor. The DJs were playing classic hip-hop – and I'd heard plenty of that already from Lady Sanity.

The Villa drew, by the way.

FOR THE MANY ...

The prospect of meeting and interviewing UB40 made me the most nervous I'd been since worrying about my wife standing me up at the altar. (Well, she IS much too good for me.) But the lads were lovely and put me right at ease ...

Back in 1979, UB40 played their first public show at the Hare and Hounds, King's Heath, a few stops on the No. 50 bus from their old Balsall Heath stomping ground. It seems like every time we go there someone is taking a photo of the plaque commemorating the legendary gig – an important early milestone on the road to becoming the biggest reggae band in the world.

They've since sold over 100 million records and spent eleven of the intervening forty years ACTUALLY IN THE CHARTS! Let that sink in for a minute. Now, fresh from a tour celebrating the fortieth anniversary of their first public outing, the Birmingham icons are back with a new album, *For the Many*. It's a vibrant, modern-sounding record containing some beautiful, heart-warming love songs and shot through with the kind of radical messages with which the band made their name.

I went to see the lads before their signing session at HMV in the Bull Ring, and collared drummer and the greatest surviving James Brown for a wide-ranging chat about their humble beginnings, the new record and some points in between.

You've had a forty-year love affair with reggae. How did you all get into it?

We're mainly from Balsall Heath and Small Heath, where a lot of Caribbean people settled, and reggae was what we heard coming from the houses and open car windows. We were already into Tamla Motown and when reggae came along it seemed a natural progression. The alternatives at the time were prog rock and glam rock, which just wasn't us – we felt that was music for middle-class students. We're obviously a multi-racial band and reggae was accessible. I wouldn't say it's easy to play but there is a certain simplicity to it, and it all just fell into place. So in a way, we didn't choose reggae – reggae chose us.

Were you all mates then?

Four of us went to Moseley School of Art together, plus the newbie, Duncan [Campbell, who replaced brother Ali on lead vocals after the band's acrimonious and well-publicised split].

Duncan himself points out the absurdity of being considered the newbie after racking up four albums and 500 shows. The lads meander down memory lane to their schooldays, with tales of stealing paint brushes from the Midland Educational shop round the corner from Oasis market ('we hid them up our sleeves'), and Jimmy reminisces about Duncan's nerves when he first took over Ali's role in the band. 'He was like a rabbit caught in headlights, which I enjoyed because he was bigger than me at school.'

'Things haven't improved for you in that situation, Jim,' says Duncan.

Jimmy continues, 'So, when Ali left, we didn't have to go outside our gang for a replacement, we kept it tight.'

It's a very fresh sounding album, it seems the split has given you a new lease of life.

It has, and not just musically. Ali wasn't happy for a good few years before he left, and when he did it was like a heavy weight being lifted from our shoulders. We play happy music; although a lot of the lyrics are political, the music is supposed to be uplifting, and it's hard to do that when there's someone with a face like a smacked arse over your shoulder. He didn't enjoy playing live, and while the rest of us would come off stage buzzing and having had a great time, he was miserable and that would bring down the vibe. We look forward to the gigs again now.

Talking of gigs, how has the new album been received by live audiences?

We've had a great reaction to it – really good. All the local artists who are guests on the record – Gilly G, Pablo Ryder and Slinger – joined us on the tour and went down a storm. They were on the Baggariddim album from '85 and just picked up where they left off, so the fans were familiar with them and welcomed them back with open arms.

Signing Off was loved by the critics, *Labour of Love* sold millions, what are you hoping for with this album?

It's a different business now – nobody sells millions anymore unless they're Ed Sheeran or the very latest thing, and most people are streaming or downloading. But we've taken more inspiration from Signing Off than Labour of Love on this one. There's plenty of dub and instrumentals breaks, five- and six-minute songs, which we haven't done for a while. We've gone full circle in terms of original songs over covers, and of course, the political message.

Has something about today's politics inspired this?

It's the same politics. If anything, what's happening today has roots in what was happening when we wrote Signing Off. The housing crisis, the banking crash – the seeds were sown by Thatcher in the eighties when she sold off the council houses and deregulated the banks. We were right then and we're right now. The frustrating thing is that a lot of it was carried on by Blair, who had a mandate to repair some of the damage of Thatcherism but didn't. As you get older you kind of give up on changing the world, but having a real Labour man like Corbyn leading the party has given us renewed hope and belief that change is possible, and it's exciting after years of just coming to terms with the idea that things would never really change.

A lot of Birmingham artists achieve barely a fraction of your success and leave. How come you've never been tempted away?

We've all got families of our own and extended family in Birmingham, and we've never played the game of being in the tabloids, being seen at the right parties, or wanting to be snapped by the paparazzi. We've still got the same mates we always had, so that keeps your feet on the ground. Also, to some degree the city informs what we do – without that influence we wouldn't sound like we do, so we feel it's important to stay.

And yet the music itself travels so well, doesn't it?

Yeah, it's unbelievable at times. A couple of years ago we went to Samoa to their independence anniversary and 20,000 turned up all singing the songs back to us. That's as far as you can go without coming back on yourself, so the music has literally gone all around the globe, and everywhere we go we get a brilliant response. For the first ten or twenty years the crowds would be cheering and we were looking round wondering who else had come on stage, until we eventually worked out the cheers were for us.

And with that the members of UB40 – supremely talented, yet refreshingly modest, fiercely working class, yet absolute gentlemen – left to hear more cheers from the people waiting for them to sign copies of the new album. It's been on repeat since I got home and if those adoring hordes want an authentic, thoughtful and pretty damned inspirational UB40 record, they won't be disappointed.

NOT THE FEW

After the interview, Jimmy kindly offered tickets to one of their shows, and I gratefully opted for the Leamington gig ...

UB40 @ THE ASSEMBLY ROOMS, LEAMINGTON SPA

Looking forward to this gig also had me looking back to the early eighties, when Birmingham ruled the charts. If Dexy's, The Beat or Duran Duran weren't on *Top of the Pops*, you could usually rely on Musical Youth or UB40 to fly our flag. And as a football fan arriving at a pub full of locals in a strange town, the best way to announce the presence of a coachload of Brummies was either to confuse everyone by asking for a pint of mild or put UB40 on the juke box. They were world famous, but undeniably ours.

They say there are six degrees of separation between any two people on earth, but it seems to me that there are zero degrees between UB40 and the people of Brum, because so many of us have a personal history that we share with them. My mate was in the 'Red Red Wine' video – he's a football coach in America now, but I still work with his brother. Another bloke at work has been sulking for decades because he reckons it was between him and Astro for a place in the band and his bitterness about not getting the gig endures.

A friend borrowed my copy of *Signing Off* to impress a girl who was coming round to his house – it obviously worked because they've stayed together longer than the original line-up and I never got it back. I bought it again of course – I named my son Tyler after the opening song – and if you haven't proudly pointed out their landmark studio in Digbeth to an out-of-towner or played pool with the band at the Oddfellows Arms in Sherlock Street, you're either too young to have done so or you're not actually a Brummie.

Yet their appeal is global. When a pal of mine met his wife in London (she is from Christchurch, New Zealand), he was into bands like PiL and The Cult and really disliked the only one she raved about – UB40. He took her to many gigs, but never to see her favourites. He promised that if ever UB40 came to Christchurch after they emigrated, he would take her to see them. He thought he'd be safe on the other side of the world, but unbeknown to him, the band had their first number one single in New Zealand and the love between the band and the Kiwi public is mutual. One day, his wife came home from work, excited that UB40 were coming over. He couldn't believe his (bad) luck but agreed to get tickets. He went along in trepidation (his idea of reggae is Steel Pulse and Yellowman), but in his words, 'I've never seen a band enjoying themselves so much and I found myself having to eat a shed-load of humble pie. It's still one of the best gigs I've been to.'

I faced a similar dilemma for the show last Friday. I love the band. I bought their first album twice, their latest one, and a few in between, and the *Labour of Love* short film is quite possibly the best thing I've ever seen, especially the bit where three Balsall Heath ladies of the night provide backing vocals on 'Many Rivers to Cross'. But my wife wasn't a fan.

This wouldn't be a problem if they were on in town and I could go on my own, but for an after-work sprint to picturesque Leamington I needed her German whip. I got round this by suggesting we get a ticket for her mum, who is an even bigger fan than me, as a Mother's Day gift, and we made it just in time to collect our tickets and take our place on the balcony at the impressive and packed-out venue.

UB40. (© STEWART LAWLEY)

The band opened with 'Here I Am (Come and Take Me)' and the tone was set. Hit after hit, encompassing all aspects of love, life and politics, received ecstatically by an adoring crowd. Any band would miss as talented a musician as Brian Travers (presently recovering from major surgery), but his protege Martin Meredith did a great job of leading a powerful brass section in the great man's absence, and Brian's last-minute replacement Ian Thompson, having learned all the songs in three days, performed his daunting task manfully.

Duncan Campbell provided flawless vocals with brother Robin doubling up as lead guitarist and master of ceremonies, while a rhythm section of Earl Falconer on bass and drummer Jimmy Brown just ran tings with fire, skill and consummate ease from the back of the stage. Tony Mullings embellished the songs with his classic reggae keyboards and Laurence Parry was a vital component of the band's signature brass sound.

Signing Off, one of the best and most important Brummie albums of all time, was well represented by 'Food For Thought', 'King' and the aforementioned 'Tyler', and we were also treated to a few from their most recent opus, *For the Many.* 'You Haven't Called' is a beautiful tale of lovelorn loneliness and a worthy addition to the UB canon. 'The Keeper' saw Robin tug at the heartstrings, while the cover of Joya Landis' 'Moonlight Lover' had percussionist Norman Hassan leading the way on vocals, ably assisted by *Baggariddim* vet Gilly G reprising his role on the recorded version from underneath a Peaky Blinders cap.

Norman continued on centre stage for 'Broken Man' from the new LP, and 'Johnny Too Bad' from *Labour of Love,* on which he threw some energetic dancehall shapes to the delight of the audience. Earl Falconer first showed off his falsetto vocals on The Heptones' 'Baby', then his toasting skills on the anti-Trump rant 'Bulldozer'. There was a touching version of Willie Nelson's 'Blue Eyes Crying in the Rain' and, just when you thought they'd run out of massive hits, they hit you with another half a dozen from what is, by any measure, an incredible back catalogue.

'Higher Ground', 'Sing our own Song', 'I'll be your Baby Tonight', 'Cherry oh Baby' … the hits just kept on coming, until a great singalong version of 'Red Red Wine' makes you think that really must be it for iconic anthems. By this time, my missus was loving it and dancing and singing along with the rest of us. It seemed like she filmed every other song on her phone and was as enthusiastic as anyone in demanding an encore. The band obliged, returning for 'One in Ten' and 'Kingston Town', before a pertinent summary of my wife's new-found feelings towards the band, 'I Can't Help Falling in Love with You', closed the two-hour party.

There are many great artists and big names who represent the city of Birmingham. From Black Sabbath to the Moody Blues, Napalm Death to Panjabi MC, our famed diversity spans the globe, while Lady Leshurr mentions the place so often she can probably make up 0121 rhymes in her sleep. UB40 are different. They look like a cross-section of the population, and their accents are so pronounced Chrissie Hynde needed interpreters to understand them. Some of them are bluenoses, some claret and blue, they've been to blues parties, they are blue collar and none of them are afraid of hard collar. They alternate between being as radical as the Birmingham Political Union and as conservative (with a small 'c') as Bournville's licensing laws. Other acts do a great job of representing the city of Birmingham; UB40 make it flesh.

UNDER PRESSURE

I'd heard of her from my sister-in-law, Olivia. I'd seen her once already at a cosy little gig. I'd even tipped her for the top in print. But I didn't really get how great she was until this …

MAHALIA @ THE CASTLE AND FALCON

I'd been counting the days to this gig from the moment I printed the tickets off weeks ago, not least because my beautiful wife Kerri was supposed to come with me. But when it became apparent that we wouldn't be able to get childcare, I had to put my foot down. Mother's Day tomorrow or not, I'm the number one Mahalia fan in our house and Wifey would be the one staying in with the kids. Translation: I begged, I pleaded, I promised to bring her breakfast in bed in the morning. Hell, I didn't even go down the Villa!

I did, however, get into town early enough to catch the last ten minutes of the game on TV in the Big Bull's Head, surrounded by Birmingham City fans who, for some unknown reason, seemed rather disgruntled at our demolition of Real Wolverhampton. For many people from outside Birmingham, Broad Street is known as the nightlife Mecca. But as a Brummie with a rock-and-roll lifestyle, I'm glad to say I hardly ever have to leave Digbeth. Aside from the odd gig at the Hare and Hounds, Weller at the NEC, or the occasional open-mic at the Bierkeller, everything I want is there: great food at Digbeth Dining Club, welcoming traditional boozers like the Old Crown, mod and Northern Soul at the Night Owl, a plethora of little venues and artists to play in them, and lots of lovely people.

Now, as local lad Samuel Johnson once nearly said, 'A man who is tired of Digbeth is tired of life', and with the spring the Villa had put in my step, I'd be lying if I told you I wasn't tempted to stay in the UK's coolest district (copyright Travel Supermarket), where I could find some mates with whom to celebrate our victory. Even if they were mostly Blues fans. I popped out onto the street for a fag and stood behind a couple of my Blues mates who weren't aware of my presence to eavesdrop on their Villa-related conversation.

'They only beat Wolves but to hear them talk you'd think they'd won the European Cup.'

I leaned in between them and said, 'What? Again?'

Staying round here was getting more tempting by the minute, especially when I saw that The Wailers were on at the Institute, but the prospect of seeing Mahalia live, albeit on my one, was even more attractive, so I hailed a No. 50 bus and headed for Balsall Heath.

Mahalia takes the stage accompanied by the affable Charlie on bass and the opening bars of 'No Pressure', a melodic yet brutal exposé of the murky world of the music industry, and an immediate sign of how her song writing has evolved in the year since I tipped her for the top in an article for music website Counteract. Further evidence of her development is provided by the fuller sound of the anthemic 'Independence Day' and the anti-bullying message of 'Silly Girl', while the utterly charming 'Marry Me' had me Googling the bigamy laws.

Up until quite recently, Mahalia has mostly written beautifully crafted stories of love-struck adolescence, but next tune 'No Reply' is the work of an emotionally articulate and strong young woman. It's probably my favourite song of the night, in spite of stiff competition from the plaintive 'Back-up Plan', a real tour de force that has the crowd singing along to the chorus.

We are then treated to a glorious mash-up of SZA's 'The Weekend' and Solange's 'Cranes in the Sky' – sung, played and arranged so perfectly it has me questioning Dobie Gray's assertion that the original is always the greatest. The meaty commercial beat of 'Hold On' is then followed, after she gets her breath back, by the rites-of-passage story 'Seventeen', which Mahalia introduces with amusing tales of fake IDs and teenage clubbing in Birmingham.

In fact, all through the set her between-song banter and audience engagement is witty, warm and erm … engaging. She then tugs at my heartstrings with another personal favourite, the absolutely gorgeous 'I Remember', a song that, when I first heard it, convinced me she was destined for greatness. She informs us that she doesn't play it very often these days, which is like a football manager saying he's signed Lionel Messi but he's only going to pick him once a month. Madness.

On first listen, new song 'Honeymoon' sounds like another winner, and after explaining that she doesn't do encores, Mahalia finishes with 'Sober', a proper grown-up song that has clocked up 7 million YouTube views and promises to be a real game-changer for her career.

So, she doesn't do encores, but she does hang around afterwards to chat and take photos with her fans, a nice touch that seemingly everyone there, including yours truly, takes advantage of and really appreciates. I somehow doubt she'll have time for all that in future, when I have no doubt whatsoever that, rather than the 300 lucky souls here tonight, she'll be playing to audiences of thousands. No Pressure, dear.

A SHARK'S TALE

2019 was a good year for B-Town originals JAWS. They released a critically acclaimed third album, played to their biggest ever crowds and had a video directed by celebrity fan Brooklyn Beckham. I was in Digbeth for the hometown leg of their nationwide tour ...

JAWS @ THE DIGBETH INSTITUTE

Along with their mates Peace and Swim Deep, JAWS were at the forefront of the B-Town scene that briefly threatened world domination in the early 2010s. After a few gigs at places like the Adam and Eve, a series of legendary performances at parties in Digbeth, and some seminal short-run singles and EPs, Peace signed a huge deal with Columbia, Swim Deep were signed by Sony/RCA, and JAWS ... well, JAWS were always the bridesmaid, never the bride.

For some reason, they never struck a major chord with a major label, or even the wider demographic that includes the likes of me, so it was with the famed nonchalance of the B-Town bands that I greeted the news that I had landed a ticket to see their show at Digbeth Institute on Saturday night. As someone who simply never shuts up about Peace (ask anyone), you can tell how little I've talked about JAWS over the years by the fact that when I told my wife I was going to see them, she thought I was off to the Mockingbird cinema for a night of shark-themed seventies nostalgia.

But something has breathed new life into the band, and with sold-out shows in Glasgow, Manchester and London behind them, JAWS attracted another capacity crowd to the hometown leg of the tour. Me and my mate Simon Pitt of the BMAs somehow managed to resist the sweet sounds emanating from DJ Sainy's Northern Soul night at the Big Bull's Head and went straight into the gig to see the band open with 'Looking/Passing' from their new album, released only a month ago but with which their loyal supporters already seemed familiar.

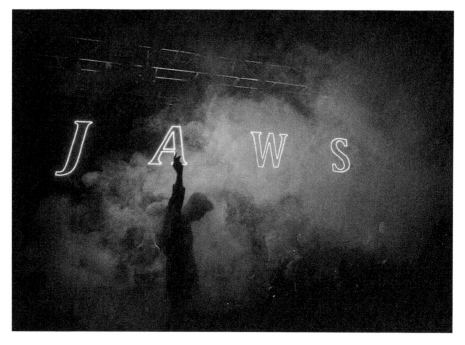

JAWS. (© PHIL DRURY, 2324 PHOTOGRAPHY)

The set was peppered with the occasional established fan favourite from their first two albums: popular B-side 'Stay in, Stay out', 'Think too Much, Feel too Little' from their debut album, and 'Right in Front of Me' from 2016's *Simplicity*, but it was the new stuff that really set the pulse racing. 'Please be Kind' is a fantastic song, a sign that the band have stopped gazing at their shoes for long enough to write an accessible chorus to go along with their introspective lyrics and thrillingly good musicianship.

Thanks to the diversity of the new album, the overall sound is more varied than it used to be; riffs that John Squire would be proud of are still there, but they alternate with fuzzier, scuzzier motifs, more reminiscent of T Rex and Slade at their best – sometimes, as in the case of the brilliant 'Do You Remember', in the same song. Front-man Connor Schofield's voice switched easily from a powerful rasp to a distant echo, depending on the mood of the song, be it the acoustic feel of January, the dream-pop of new album title track 'The Ceiling', or the pulsating drum and bass-propelled rock of 'Driving at Night'. Things got all wavy and ravey on the ultra-modern trance-pop of 'Feel' and its near neighbour, 'Fear', and the crowd responded in kind, generating the kind of energy that would save the planet if it could be harnessed to the national grid.

The band played eight tracks from the new LP, and I can honestly say I've never been so impressed by a collection of songs I've never heard before. They had at least one guaranteed sale, no doubt whatsoever, and from the crowd reaction everybody else had already bought it. The main set finished with the title track from their debut album, *Be Slowly*, and although most of the audience and band don't look old enough to remember it, we couldn't let them go without revisiting the heady days of 2013 anthem, 'Gold', if only to give someone in the crowd a chance to let off their last smoke bomb.

I walked out as a fan, clutching a copy of *The Ceiling* and trying to find out about the after-party. Barry Nicholson of the *NME* summed up the B-Town phenomenon better than I ever could, and over half a decade later, I'm still jealous of his prose, 'Some scenes come roaring out of the traps; B-Town seemed to roll out of bed, insular and uncontrived, smirking at its own in-jokes, smelling faintly of K cider and intent on nothing loftier than the pursuit of a laugh.'

JAWS have grown up a lot since then, and although they might still be in pursuit of a laugh, this was the kind of performance that forces you to take them seriously.

DAVID CAMERON, WAYNE ROONEY AND ME

With only a few days left until the biggest night in the local music calendar, I went looking for clues and a catch-up with a local legend …

It's the week of the Birmingham Music Awards, and the quirky bars and coffee shops of Brum's Bohemia are alive with hype and gossip about who will win and who will attend. Me and my missus have tickets for the VIP area – she leaves the jeans-and-trainers-type gigs to me and the kids but show her a red carpet and a champagne reception and she's organising childcare quicker than Amazon Prime can deliver a new dress. At £85 a ticket, I'm out to impress her, and I've been with her long enough to know that, along with some free Prosecco, what will impress her most is if Lady Leshurr turns up.

My mates Simon Pitt and Jo Jeffries are running the show, but they won't tell me, so I'm left with no alternative but to find out from as close to the horse's mouth as I can get. I've met quite a few of the Birmingham music scene's movers and shakers over the years, but none of them move and shake quite like George 'G-Jiggy' Francis. Born in Moseley, he emigrated to Jamaica, aged 4, where he won a singing competition broadcast live on national TV. At 13, he came back to his birth city after the sudden death of his father, and attended Smethwick Hall Boys School. At some point after that, he bought himself a video camera – and boy did he use it.

As a videographer and editor, he's worked for Alexander McQueen, Sony, Gucci, Sean Paul, Julian Marley, Wu Tang Clan, Jesse Jackson, UB40 and, as I call him, David Bloody Cameron. And if you're Wayne Rooney, who do get to get do your wedding video? G-Jiggy of course! He also runs the IDA UK and Ireland DJ organisation and has managed and mentored world champion 'turntablists' such as Italian superstar DJ Mandrayk.

At the age of 51, he thought it was about time he had some letters after his name and got a BSc (Hons) in Film Production Technology from Staffordshire University – his lifetime of hands-on experience meant they couldn't teach him much and he graduated from the four-year degree in just eighteen months. He's helped out the West Midlands Combined Authority at the global property expo

MIPIM, won awards for services to the community, and has had two films nominated at the Birmingham Film Festival.

We met up at the White Room in the Custard Factory and I steered the conversation towards all things Leshurr.

I first saw her at a showcase event for unsigned acts in 2006 and when she started rapping it gave me goosebumps. I told her there and then she would be massive, but she took some convincing. Three months later she won a female MC of the year award but was still miserable about the prospect of 9–5 work. She just wanted to do music but didn't have the resources. I believed in her and had my own business, so it was easy for me to go to Major Studios in Brum and tell them – I want you to let this girl use the studio whenever she wants for as long as she wants. One night I picked her up from there after she had recorded a track, from start to finish, in 45 minutes. It was called 'Slow Flow' and trust me, the title is ironic. She put it on in the car and it blew me away and convinced me I had backed a winner. There's also a correlation there with my relationship with Lady Sanity, who I advised in 2017 just three months before she won a prestigious Get Rated award.

What have you been up to outside music?

I've worked on the big Netflix series Sex Education and the remake of Dumbo, and I'm currently doing a bit for a new BBC series called His Dark Materials, that's on later this year. I'm also working on the launch this summer of fashion and make-up brands GJIGGY and Streetlife Boutique, mentoring young people and doing artist and model management. It's all about using the huge talent pool in the West Midlands and keeping it all local so that Birmingham thrives. I'm an 0121 foot-soldier.

Talking of the West Midlands, you've been helping out the combined authority, haven't you?

Yes, I was part of a big team that went to Cannes for MIPIM, where we showcased to the world all the investment opportunities across the region. I know they get a bad rap but people like Andy Street are doing a fantastic job, in my opinion. He was doing presentations, introductions, then he'll be behind the scenes talking to investors, then making a keynote speech. I was filming him for twelve hours straight and never saw him stop for so much as a sandwich. It was a real eye-opener to have the inside track on how much is going on in Birmingham, and believe me, after the Commonwealth Games and all the stuff around HS2 is finished in 2026 the whole world will wanna come here.

On that optimistic note, we parted, and I remembered why I'd arranged to meet him in the first place. I text him on my way home, 'So, is Leshurr coming to the Birmingham Music Awards or not?'

To which he replied, 'Well, she's booked a table for eight in the VIP area, but you'll have to wait and see if she's one of the eight.'

I'm taking my selfie stick just in case.

AFFIEJAM. (STEPHEN PENNELL)

ERIN GRACE. (© PAUL MOREAU)

MAHALIA AT THE CASTLE AND FALCON. (STEPHEN PENNELL)

LADY LESHURR, KERRI PENNELL AND KURTIS. (KERRI PENNELL)

SIMON PITT, CONNOR SCHOFIELD AND STEPHEN PENNELL AT THE CASTLE AND FALCON. (SIMON PITT)

PAUL COOK — FOUNDER OF THE SUNFLOWER LOUNGE. (STEPHEN PENNELL)

PEAKY BLINDERS TOUR. (STEPHEN PENNELL)

PHIL ETHERIDGE – THE TWANG. (KERRI PENNELL)

PAUL WELLER. (STEPHEN PENNELL)

THE CLAUSE. (© LUKE JONES)

REVELLERS AT THE NIGHT OWL. (KERRI PENNELL)

TIM SENNA. (JODIE RICHARDS)

UB40 PLAQUE. (STEPHEN PENNELL)

TYDAL AND GHETTS. (STEPHEN PENNELL)

BIRMINGHAM AT ITS MUSICAL BEST

THE BIRMINGHAM MUSIC AWARDS @ THE MILL, DIGBETH

The tickets weren't cheap – VIP gold class and all that jazz. The accompanying email said arrive at 6 p.m. in a rather assertive way and I thought we'd better comply. So I was a bit miffed as my wife Kerri and I were still in the queue in a draughty and chilly Lower Trinity Street at quarter past six. She looked gorgeous as ever, like Olivia Pope going clubbing, but her hair was blowing all over the place and the little bit I've got left was trying its best to get messy.

Don't get me wrong – I've spent entire weekends out in the cold on Lower Trinity Street, flitting between Mama Roux's, the Night Owl and Digbeth Dining Club, but always either fully anaesthetised by alcohol or wrapped up in a fishtail parka. Tonight, neither was the case, and my mood wasn't helped when a few people I vaguely recognised walked straight to the front and were allowed in. On my own, I'm not precious about stuff like that, but as my missus often says, 'Happy wife, happy life' … and she wasn't happy.

I approached the bouncers and threw my press credentials at them, hinting that they were going to get written about. That did the trick and they let us in and … whoops! … I've written about them anyway.

The first drinks were free and the rest were lovely, so having recovered from the hangover, I'm now battling against a drunken haze to let you know what else happened at the second annual Birmingham Music Awards, ready to drop more names than Preditah drops beats. As we lined up for our VIP passes, we bumped into post-punk politicos The Novus, one of the most promising bands in Brum, who invited us to the next in their series of secret location gigs in September. 'Where at?' I asked, making an early play for the 'silliest question' award.

Then another two of my favourites, Luke Henry and B of CityLightz, came over, and I introduced them to Kerri. 'Punching above your weight there, aren't you?' said B, and much as I wanted to punch him, I had to agree. After chatting to Michael out of Karkosa and bowing, scraping and going weak in the presence of greatness as I spoke to Steve Ajao, we went up to the intimate VIP area, only realising halfway up the stairs that we were climbing them with Lady Leshurr and her entourage. I also saw Remtrex, who once caused much controversy by recording a song and YouTube video while locked up in Winson Green. 'Best not to bother him,' I thought.

Host Alex Noble from BBC WM *Introducing* ... erm ... introduced himself. He did a brilliant job all night – efficient, slick, witty, hilarious at times, particularly when begrudgingly handing over awards for which he himself was nominated.

Sugarthief opened the live performances with one from their new EP and B-town 2.0 anthem, 'Joy Affair', followed by Relley C with her song 'Priceless', to which Lady Sanity brought the flames. Community project winners The Choir With No Name gave a rousing rendition of Tears For Fears' 'Shout', and Namywa put on the performance of the night with 'Jungle', backed by her brilliant band and dancers.

While presenting the Best Male award, Andy McCluskey of OMD voiced his admiration for the show, and his jealousy that Liverpool has no equivalent. Other highlights were rocking good shows by Fuzzbox, The Nu and Riscas, and bumping into The Clause by the bar.

It may be a bit early into their career for them to be scooping up all the awards, but their day will come – remember, I told you. If there was a best-dressed category, they'd have walked it.

After a rambling, bizarre, brilliantly entertaining and maximum rock-and-roll speech by Steve Gibbons, the Lifetime Achievement award brought back happy memories of seeing the recipient, Trevor Burton, live at the Boulton Arms in Small Heath, on the very night the rest of the world was watching U2 fanning their fame with famine on Live Aid. Amazing to think that with a slight kink in music history, it could have been Trevor and the rest of The Move on that Wembley stage.

It was nice to see Brian Travers honoured with the Brum Bastion award, although his recent health problems prevented him from appearing in person. Happily, I hear he is well on the road to recovery. Several awards had a nice personal resonance for me. I first saw Best Rap/Grime act Lady Leshurr performing as part of a trio with my daughter at a school concert; Best Male, Dapz On The Map, is a close family friend; my favourite club the Night Owl won Best Club Night for Le Freak; Call Me Unique and Lady Sanity (along with Namywa and AffieJam) are my reason and inspiration for writing about music; and my son's mate, Mayday, won a great package of career help from main sponsors CD Baby after being voted Rising Star.

The evening was rounded off in style with two songs from JAWS, who won Best Band for the second year running. It was a great night out, but more than that, it was a platform for local talent, a celebration of our culture and diversity, rare recognition for those behind the scenes, a great idea by the Birmingham Film Festival's Dean Williams, and brilliantly realised by Jo Jeffries and Simon Pitt.

With 750 people in attendance, all those live performances, thirty-six categories of award, a presenter or two for each one, a winner or a band or an entourage or a choir for each one … it must have been a logistical nightmare, and yet it was all carried off with barely a hitch. As proceedings came to an end, I was a bit gutted that our childcare didn't stretch to the after-party at Mama Roux's, but I'll just have to make do with the free monthly events the BMAs put on throughout the year. The tickets weren't cheap, but they were the best value for money I've had in many a year. Roll on, 2020.

SUGARTHIEF. (© LUKE JONES)

THE GREAT HANDOVER

The day Birmingham started limbering up for the 2022 Commonwealth Games …

LADY SANITY, DANIEL ALEXANDER, AMERAH SALEH, ROSIE KAY @ THE COMMONWEALTH GAMES HANDOVER CEREMONY. (VENUES: THE GOLD COAST, A BIRMINGHAM LIVING ROOM, VICTORIA SQUARE AND THE SUNFLOWER LOUNGE)

Although I was scheduled to do my normal Sunday morning overtime, I'd informed the gaffer the previous week that I'd be foregoing a few hours double time by leaving early so I could watch the Birmingham segment of the Commonwealth Games handover ceremony, to be broadcast live from Australia to a TV audience of billions. There was a bit of a fright when my cable TV went down the day before, and although I'm not going to advertise who my provider is, suffice it to say that after posting a threatening tweet to Richard Branson it was soon up and running again in time for the big day.

For the most part, the ceremony from Australia was awful, and I was beginning to think I should have stayed at work for an extra few quid. A host of nondescript singers performed generic, sub-*X-Factor*-style dirges as a prelude to a seemingly endless round of dull speeches, and I was having trouble justifying my iron grip on the remote control to the kids, who would have much preferred to be watching *Peppa Pig*. And at that point, so would I. But then the commentator said, 'Come on Birmingham, wake everybody up!' and it was our turn.

We opened with a short video, a light-hearted but accurate reflection of the city in its honesty, diversity and self-deprecating humour. Set to the banging beat of Lotto Boyzz' 'Birmingham Anthem', we saw Spaghetti Junction, the Bull Ring markets, grime star Jaykae dressed as a Peaky Blinder, and the film's producer, Jewellery Quarter-based Daniel Alexander, getting vexed with one of his actors. We're so self-effacing, we even left the bloopers in.

Then it was back to the Gold Coast for a live performance. For this, the stars had aligned sometime in 2017. First, Durban's proposed hosting of the

Commonwealth Games in 2022 collapsed due to lack of finance, and Birmingham stepped into the breach by beating Liverpool in the battle to take over.

Meanwhile, somewhere in Erdington, a talented young rapper was writing a song for an EP that was to come out later that year, the lyrics intensely personal, yet also resonant for any aspiring achiever (an athlete, maybe?), or a traditionally looked-down-upon city taking its well-deserved place on the world stage. Like Birmingham, the rhymes were alive with creativity, skill, energy and hard work, yet simultaneously wracked with self-doubt – 'Sometimes I wonder why it's me they put their faith in'.

Ultimately though, the song tells of a steely determination to achieve greatness, whatever the odds, whether the necessary support is there or not. It could be about the city of Birmingham, or its perfect representative, the song's writer and performer, who was now centre stage – Lady Sanity – either one fits the narrative. I was nervous as a kitten for her as she began rapping, but I needn't have worried. She was word perfect, from the opening bars to the infectious chorus at the end, and by then, the only person who was stressed out was the poor subtitles typist at the BBC, charged with the impossible task of keeping up with Sanity's machine-gun delivery.

The location then switched to our magnificent Town Hall, where Stratford Road wordsmith, Amerah Saleh treated us to a stirring reading of her poem 'Tourist in my City'. 'Birmingham – you stayed back too long,' she said, before speaking passionately on our history of protest, activism and inclusivity. Articulate as she was, there was no gloss on her words, no sense of a city pretending to be something it's not. The *Guardian*'s live blog gushed, 'This is inspiring, incendiary stuff. She's talking about Yemen, fist raised, and she means it.' I must have got something in my eye.

Amerah then led us outside into Victoria Square for the big finale, a dance performed perfectly by hundreds of young Brummies and choreographed brilliantly by another one, Rosie Kay, to the backing of ELO's 'Mr Blue Sky'. It was a triumph of organisation and a joyful conclusion to our bit of the closing ceremony. I enjoyed it so much that I went to Victoria Square the following Saturday to see homecoming queen, Sanity reprise her performance (marvellous again), and got the chance to congratulate in person the utterly charming Amerah Saleh on her reading of her poem.

As if to prove Amerah's point about Birmingham's history of activism, Sanity's performance was almost interrupted by marchers protesting against the scandalous treatment of the Windrush generation. And more power to them – I was torn between staying near the stage and joining the protest. After that, it was home to drop off 6-year-old Lewis, who was fed up with the rain, and 7-year-old Amber, who already has a published poem and an ambition to be the next Lady Sanity, and get myself back out to the Sunflower Lounge to see a proper Sanity gig.

She was impressive as always but, with typical Brummie contrariness, she didn't do her now best-known tune. I hope she's not sick of it because, I'll wager, she'll be performing it a lot over the next four years. There will be ups and downs in that time, with lots of big projects for the games organising committee to get to grips with, but if ever I feel it might all go wrong, I'll just remember the closing bars of 'Go the Distance':

In a world full of cannots, let me tell you that you are astounding,
And I'd rather a handful of hope than a future of doubting.

GUEST STARRING – NEW YORK

A trip to the second-greatest city on earth, with thoughts of the first never far from my mind …

I must have been all loved up when my mate announced on Facebook that, through his links with Anthony Joshua's Brummie trainer, Rob McCracken, he had got hold of 200 tickets for AJ's US debut at Madison Square Garden. My wife Kerri loves AJ, which is understandable when one look at me tells you that he is just her type. I've often toyed with the idea of taking her to one of his fights instead of paying £20 for her to watch him on the telly. With loads of my mates going, this seemed like a perfect chance for an exciting city break and, as ever, Kerri organised our travel plans with military precision.

The outbound journey via Gatwick passed off with barely a hitch, although there was one frightening moment when immigration officials split us up at JFK, but I somehow managed to get through security alone without having to throw myself at the mercy of the British Embassy. After a much-needed night's sleep at our hotel on Eighth Avenue and a ravenous raid on the breakfast buffet, we were ready to take in the sights and sounds of the second-greatest city on earth, armed with nothing more than a fistful of dollars, a couple of tickets for the boxing, and a Groupon voucher, bought online at home, which provided us with a list as long as Livery Street of pre-paid attractions and activities.

First off, we got a two-day ticket for the hop-on, hop-off Big Bus Tour, and … erm … hopped on. After seeing much of the sun-drenched city from the upper deck, we alighted at the stunning memorial to the victims of 9/11, Ground Zero. It was every bit as moving as you might imagine, especially the tradition of placing a rose next to the names of the lost whose birthdays fall on that particular day. It's a spectacular, worthy tribute, and one that causes a tinge of regret – a feeling that we've done a disservice to the victims of the Birmingham pub bombings by allowing the Tavern in the Town to become a nondescript pizza restaurant instead of something more fitting.

From Ground Zero, it was little more than a brisk walk to the pier, where we boarded the ferry that gets you up close and personal to the Statue of Liberty and

Ellis Island. The on-board commentary was informative and entertaining and, in the age of Trump, it was heartening to hear that some Americans are still proud of the welcoming attitude towards immigrants that the statue, a gift from France to the US, represents. It may seem obvious to the practical types amongst you, but I was surprised to learn that Lady Liberty arrived in flat-pack form with assembly required. Can you imagine the instructions?

We then enjoyed (endured?) a cross-town ride on the crowded subway, on which I asked a native New Yorker for the best stop to get off for 42nd Street, which is near our hotel. She just smiled and said, '42nd Street'.

The last leg of our first full day in the Big Apple was spent in Times Square, where we bought a few bits and pieces from the Levi's shop at around midnight. The square and surrounding streets were packed with people until the early hours, and we spent an interesting ten minutes watching a homeless man having a heated debate with himself as he enjoyed a big plate of spaghetti and meatballs from off the top of a rubbish bin.

The day of the fight began with a peaceful few hours walking round Central Park, six and a half times the size of Hyde Park, according to a bloke who wanted to take us round on his bicycle taxi. He was obviously eager to impress and/or make his service seem necessary; he wasn't to know I'm from a biophilic city of 571 parks, one of which is the biggest urban one in Europe.

Small as Central Park is compared to ours in Sutton, we still couldn't find the Diana Ross Playground or the John Lennon tribute, Strawberry Fields, although we did come across a bloke proposing to his girlfriend. She said 'yes', accompanied by applause and cheers from those around when, as someone who has only witnessed public proposals at Villa Park, I half expected to hear a chorus of 'You don't know what you're doing' from the onlookers.

Then it was back on the bus for my personal highlight of the trip, a visit to Harlem. On the way, we passed some of the most celebrity-laden areas of the city; the neighbourhood where Allen Ginsberg and Jack Kerouac hung around together and the spots where Lennon lived and died, quickly followed by the home of his killer's inspiration, J.D. Salinger. Our guide said he'd seen the Beatle's widow out walking a few weeks ago, and after hearing that, we kept our eyes peeled for a bit of Yoko-spotting, sadly to no avail.

If ever I think about what New York means to me, my first and last thought is music, so Harlem was a must see. The guide abandoned his commentary halfway round and treated us to a soundtrack of Duke Ellington, Bill Withers, James Brown and, of course, Bobby Womack as we drove down 110th Street. We saw the Martin Luther King and Malcolm X Boulevards, the hotel where Malcolm met a young boxer called Clay and persuaded him to change his name, and the building where the radical leader was assassinated, just days after making his last speech outside the US – in Birmingham. The guide for this tour was a white bloke, but he spoke eloquently and emotively about the cultural and political impact of the district. I would have made a tearful show of myself were it not for my Ray-Bans.

After a flying visit to see Kerri's cousin at work in Macy's (the world's largest store, but the world's largest Primark in Brum must run it close), we toured the Rockefeller Center and took in the famous skyline from its observatory. Later in our trip, we took in the same views from atop the Empire State Building, which just about edges it. The building drips with history and art deco class in a way that the former doesn't, and unlike the Rockefeller, allows you to take in the spectacular views without the spoiler of Perspex sheets keeping you safe. Plus I'm a big fan of the original *King Kong* movie, so it was no contest for me.

We watched the Champions League final on our hotel room TV – it was broadcast live with Spanish commentary – but it soon became apparent it was a bit of a snooze-fest, and at half-time we headed for Madison Square Garden early to soak up the atmosphere and witness the undercard. There was boisterous support for the Brits on the bill, who had mixed fortunes, and then it was time for the main event.

Joshua's defeat was disappointing, but it was such a small part of our trip that it didn't spoil it to any great extent. As Kerri said, 'Win or lose, I could still see his muscles.' Even I couldn't see mine – my appeal is 'more cerebral' apparently.

Our itinerary was so packed that the only time I saw my mates from Brum was at the fight, where some of them were getting a bit too wound up for comfort as an American behind us sarcastically shouted, 'The British are coming!' as AJ took his beating, but overall the Limeys in the crowd accepted defeat with good grace. Most people we spoke to thought that Andy Ruiz deserved his victory – he may not have looked the part, but he certainly had the heart.

The next day started with a huge unplanned walking tour of the city as we attempted to find a gluten-free restaurant, Friedman's, that my wheat-intolerant wife had spotted on Instagram. It was a lot harder to find in real life. When we finally thought we were in the right vicinity, we asked directions and were told that we were actually on the wrong side of town. Then, a ride in a big yellow taxi had to be abandoned as part of the route was closed to traffic for a couple of colourful parades, but that didn't stop the driver charging us $8 for a 500-yard drive in a circle.

We eventually found the place and, despite having to stop at a pharmacy to buy an ankle support, it was worth every painful step. We left them a good tip and a plea to open a branch in Brum. In the evening, we tried to book tickets to the Temptations' jukebox musical on Broadway, but it was sold out, as were all the other shows. Apparently, Tuesday is the only night of the week where one can buy tickets on a whim, so book ahead if that's your thing.

After our marathon walk and hearty Sunday dinner at Friedman's, we went back to the hotel, lay on the bed for a little breather while it poured down with rain, and woke up at about 2 a.m. The city may never sleep, but it's bloody tiring for the people.

Monday was home time, and we went shopping around Times Square for gifts for friends and family. I managed to crowbar Kerri out of the Swarovski shop ('There's one in the Bull Ring!' I reminded her, as if we're not both overly familiar with it), but we walked past it again a few times before I noticed that Wifey and the assistant in there were exchanging waves and knowing looks. In the end, I gave in and bought her some earrings.

While we were in there, Mahalia's new song came on the radio and I was proud to tell the assistant, who remarked on my caterwauling along, that the singer went to school in Birmingham with my wife's little sister. As far as I can recall, it was one of five English songs we heard on the radio while we were there: Oasis, Adele, Black Sabbath and UB40 were the others. More reminders of home came in the form of a Longbridge-built Mini, the ACME Thunderer whistles constantly blown by NYPD traffic officers, carbonated drinks and some bloke called Benjamin Franklin, who's on the dollars and was connected to the Lunar Society.

After a last supper at another branch of Friedman's restaurant, our taxi driver talked endlessly about endless traffic all the way back to JFK, where the departure lounges were in chaos. It strikes me that instead of having eight terminals and not enough gates, the airport would be more efficient with less of the former and more of the latter. I advised one particularly highly strung officer to relax, to which he barked, 'I AM RELAXED!' I'd hate to see him when he's stressed out.

Overall, it was a fantastic trip to a wonderful city with a lovely companion. (Note to editor: she'll read this, you know.) Our hotel, the Hampton on Eighth Avenue, was clean, comfortable and an oasis of calm not too far from the madding crowd. The Big Apple is no country for young kids – too crowded for them, I reckon – and some of my mates were bored because all they did was drink in bars and go to the boxing and a rounders game at Yankee Stadium. But if you like the hustle and bustle of a super-diverse city, steeped in history and culture, it's perfect. And if you don't … what are you doing in Birmingham?

EVERYTHING'S GOING SWIMMINGLY

Home again …

SWIM DEEP @ THE SUNFLOWER LOUNGE

The Sunflower Lounge, hailed by Noel Gallagher as the best venue in Britain for aspiring rock-and-roll stars, lived up to the hype this week as Swim Deep played a three-night residency under the banner '0121 Desire'. It's been four years since their last album and they've gone through some line-up changes on the long road to their new one, *Emerald Classics*.

In the meantime, a host of exciting young local bands have been tearing around town with all the verve of their inspirational forebears, and contemporaries Peace and JAWS have both released stunningly good albums recently. So, it would be great if the other third of B-Town's holy trinity came up with the goods, and the signs are promising. Frontman Ozzy Williams says it is their 'Brummiest album yet', and to prove his point, it's named after a Small Heath boozer (down Coventry Road, turn left into Green Lane, follow your nose and the Emerald is on your right).

So, here we are on the second night of the three, and I was spoiled for choice. I already had a pass out from She Who Must Be Obeyed for the Birmingham Music Awards' monthly shindig at Mama Roux's and Wednesday is a big night at Snobs, but after getting a series of excitable (and it turned out entirely justified) late-night text messages from a mate, raving about Tuesday's gig, I fired off some frantic emails and tweets until I managed to snag a ticket for the Sunny.

It wasn't exactly last minute, but I was still panicking at teatime when somebody finally came through for me. By the time I got there, Connor Schofield from JAWS was on the decks, The Twang were on the guestlist, Tim Senna from BBC WM and Switch Radio was filming one of his legendary vlogs, Kieran, the ex-football hooligan and poet, was in the blazing area and the beautiful dancing girls from round the corner at Adult World were on a celebratory night out. It could only have been more peak Birmingham if Genie Mendez out of Lycio was still working behind the bar, Eddie Fewtrell was on the door and Lee Child had Jack Reacher abseiling down the Rotunda to the gig.

I showed my e-ticket (check out thoroughly-modern-me) and rather than attack me with a stamp, the doorman drew Swim Deep's aqua sign logo on the back of my hand with a felt-tip pen. A nice touch, but it must have been a bit of a pain by the time he'd done 200 punters, three nights on the trot.

Support was provided by Tall Stories from Stourbridge, a punky yet melodic three-piece, who went down well with the packed house, particularly when they played their new single 'Lost In Translation', which may or may not be about the travails of people from the Black Country making themselves understood in the great metropolis next door.

The headliners opened with their new jam 'To Feel Good', the story of 'a day in the life of a heavyweight loser', complete with a heavyweight beat and a (sampled) gospel choir reinventing Rozalla's 'Everybody's Free'. The glory days of the initial B-Town surge were revisited with 'Honey' from the band's debut album, *Where the Heaven are we?*, and their sophomore album *Mothers* was mined for 'To My Brother' and 'One Great Song and I Could Change the World'. The big chorus of 'Sail Away, Wave Goodbye' augurs well for the new album, before a trio of old favourites, 'Soul Trippin'', 'The Sea' and 'Namaste' whipped the crowd into a state of near delirium.

SWIM DEEP. (© LUKE JONES)

The sound would be familiar to early nineties veterans (or should that be casualties?) of the Ship Ashore, the Hummingbird and Burberrys, or fans of Spin, Paris Angels, Flowered Up and Saint Etienne. It was a heady and hedonistic mix of rave, funk, chopped-up rhythms and subtle melodies from Ozzy on vocals, driven by the blood-shaking bass of ex-Peace merchandise seller, Cavan McCarthy, and Tom Tomaski on drums, while Robbie Wood on guitar and keys and James Balmont on synths and backing vocals added panoramic soundscapes with a flourish.

'Fueiho Boogie' was a sort of motorik sprawl, during which the band resembled a class of 6-year-olds, high on e-numbers, running amok unsupervised in the school music room. There are two lead guitars on the go, tambourines flying through the air and more keyboards than Sparky's Piano Shop, and the band zigzag around the stage, everybody having a bash on everything. Yes, the crowd were loving it, but you should have seen the band!

After a supercharged version of epic love song 'She Changes the Weather', Swim Deep closed the show with the ultimate B-Town anthem, 'King City'. The lyrics are inspirational, aspirational and optimistic, common themes throughout the show and a perfect summary of the band's message and, by the look of it, their state of mind. Ozzy said, 'There's never been a better time to be in Swim Deep,' and I would add that there's never been a better time to see and hear them either.

It was a beautiful night, and one for which I owe thanks and praises to Phil Etheridge for the selfie, George Whittle for the ticket, and my mate Chris Waldron, who gave me the kick up the backside I needed with his text message review of the previous night. But most of all, thanks to Swim Deep for coming home.

MAKING THE STARS ALIGN

The *Unstoppable Rise of Birmingham Rap*, Mike Skinner's self-explanatory online documentary, showed that with the likes of Jaykae, Mist and Lady Leshurr on the firm, the second city is ready, willing and able to take on the world – and win. That's perfect if you're a local music fan and gig-goer, with a diary packed with headline hometown shows and a phone full of selfies from chance meetings in the Bullring. Probably not so great when you're an up-and-coming MC, trying to stand out from the crowd and grinding hard to follow in their illustrious footsteps.

One such talent is Stardom, brought up in the mean streets of Aston, now making rapid progress towards the top of the rap food chain. His SBTV *Better Places* video on the subject of Aston and Lozells flagged him up as one to watch, and soon afterwards invites from the likes of Tim Westwood, Charlie Sloth and Kenny Allstar at Radio 1XTRA began to flood his inbox. Debut album *Grams and Dreams* was a searing commentary on inner-city street life – hard hitting, gritty and, above all, authentic – a body of work that heralded the arrival of a major talent.

Now the budget has grown and the bling has followed, on visuals for 'Shoebox Money' and certified club banger 'Gucci', and with new single 'La Vida Loca' and an EP to follow, Stardom looks set to join the ranks of rap royalty as the views and streams accelerate faster than the cars in his videos. I caught up with the new sensation of Road Rap to check on his progress.

When and how did you start rapping?

I started making music when I was about 13. My big brother used to do it so I kind of followed his lead and started myself. I've always been around it.

Who was your inspiration on a general and local level and why them in particular?

A group called B6 Slash LOZ, who were from my area and had been doing it for a while. I always looked up to them and they definitely inspired me to get where I am today.

Grams and Dreams is a great album, you must be really proud of it?

Thank you! Yeah, I think it is my best work to date as a whole. I have a lot more coming and a lot of material ready, so I keep improving.

'La Vida Loca' is a really catchy club track. Can we expect more like this in the future?

Yeah, I have a couple of catchy similar vibe tunes ready to go. The club is where music is heard most so I want to make sure I'm filling up the clubs across the UK with my music. Everyone can enjoy and catch a vibe to it.

The collaborations you've done in the past, especially on Grams and Dreams, are brilliant. Do you have any more interesting collabs coming up?

I have a couple of big names coming up. I don't want to let the cat out of the bag just yet, so stay tuned, but my next release will include a feature with an artist I rate highly.

You rap on the intro (to _Grams and Dreams_), 'I'm too Road, hey won't play me on the radio'. Would you consider toning down the harsh reality of that record to get air play, or would that be too much of a compromise and/or damage your credibility?

I think in the sense of toning it down, I have done a bit, but I think you can still get your point across in different ways, without people feeling intimidated or thinking it's too 'gangsta'. But no, that won't damage my credibility.

Your track 'Arhh Yeah' has very cinematic visuals. Is this something you'd like to develop further?

Yes, I have something I'm working on right now that I will probably drop in the next couple of months. It's the same kind of vibe as that, a mini film. I like to be creative, and I think it's important as an artist to show all sides of your creativity.

Will you be taking the new record, 'La Vida Loca', out on the road? I noticed you've done a few performances abroad.

Yes, hopefully we can get some shows and get it out there! I've done some great shows this summer across Europe and it was received really well so I want to keep that momentum in the UK and show the fans how I work live.

Is there anybody out there in Brum that you rate and want to mention?

Brum is firing right now. I rate Reeks, A1 and Blakka – if you don't know these guys, get to know. And of course Jaykae.

Somebody a lot cleverer than me could probably make a deep and meaningful point about post-millennial music consumption and how an artist with YouTube views and Spotify streams measured in the millions can still be described as 'under the radar'. But Stardom is putting in the hard yards and hard bars to change that, and my money is on him to succeed.

WORKING LAUNCH

THE CLAUSE, IN MY ELEMENT LAUNCH PARTY @ THE SUNFLOWER LOUNGE

The Clause launch their new single in triumphant style, proving that they're the new kings of Birmingham's indie scene. (A few months later, largely on the strength of this record, they'd been signed by Universal ...)

There's a certain symmetry to the choice of venue for the launch of this latest banger from The Clause. The video was filmed over the road in Snobs, where back in the nineties DJ Paul Cook put on his legendary Sunflower nights, named in honour of the Paul Weller song that heralded the onset of Britpop. When Cookie decided to open his own venue in Smallbrook Queensway, the name came with him, and now the only band in Britain as well-dressed as the Modfather are launching their new single there.

The Clause are the one band I'd go drinking and shopping with. Bassist Johnny is a world champion at smoking outside pubs and lead guitarist Liam has immaculate dress sense. They're definitely the only band I'd go to Millwall away with on a Wednesday night – drummer Niall has got the guns and front-man Pearce has perfected the thousand-yard stare.

The band have built up a loyal fanbase over the last couple of years, and many of them are here to welcome the new tune and see Pearce take over on the Sunny's wheels of steel for the night. He plays an ice-cool selection of mod, Northern Soul, Britpop and indie, but there's one tune we're here to hear above all others – their new single, 'In My Element'. He finally gives it an airing at about ten o'clock, and even though it follows on from a set list that includes the likes of T. Rex and the Rolling Stones, this is most definitely NOT a case of 'after the Lord Mayor's show'.

It starts with a hint of trance, reminiscent of the pulse of a heart monitor, underneath a Duane-Eddy-on-steroids riff. It's almost delicate, compared to what's to come, when another guitar explodes out of the speakers like a defibrillator applying a life-giving charge, or like Tony Iommi has smashed through the big front window of the Sunny on a heavy-metal wrecking ball.

The thud of drums and bass actually sends ripples through my beer – and we're off. Some bands keep you hanging on, but The Clause ain't messing about, hitting you with the chorus straight away. 'I feel a rush of blood,' sings Pearce, before listing more drug references than your average episode of *Breaking Bad*, and the guitars alternate between sounding like John Squire at his best and Sly Stone tap-dancing on a wah-wah pedal. Niall's drums and Johnny's elastic bass line carry a Stone Roses vibe, and it's no surprise that 'Fool's Gold' gets a nod in the lyrics.

During the verses the lead guitar is understated, but you can still hear it in the mix – a mollified pit bull straining at the leash until a crackle of bared teeth and growling electricity sounds a warning – watch out, the chorus is coming back! – before it breaks free and savages your ears even more brutally than it did on the intro. The twin guitars finally pause for breath, leaving the way clear for a

THE CLAUSE. (© PHIL DRURY, 2324 PHOTOGRAPHY)

stripped-back drum and bass interlude, along with some mantric vocals – 'always be in your element/ain't got time for your sentiments'.

The final guitar solo is a real string-bender and, as if there isn't enough going on, the last couple of choruses are embellished with tambourine and a swirling glitterball of disco synths, leading to more electronica and an emergency-stop finish. It's so good I struggle to describe it without swearing, and it's not just me.

It's been named as track of the month on BBC WM, and will no doubt get plenty of airplay on Brum Radio, but it's making waves outside Birmingham too – it's already on heavy rotation on Punk Aristocrats Radio 1 in Los Angeles, and it went in at No. 1 on the iTunes rock chart. If the band can keep writing and performing at this level, it's elementary that The Clause are destined for greatness.

'JAM' PACKED

A potentially bad day turns into a good one, and ends with me falling even deeper under the spell of …

AFFIEJAM @ THE SUNFLOWER LOUNGE

It all started badly a few weeks ago, when a letter arrived informing me of a hospital appointment on the afternoon of 15 May. Worse still, when I checked I discovered that I was supposed to be working the late shift and needed to book time off, using up the meagre remains of my annual leave just for the pleasure of being poked and prodded at the QE. Then AffieJam announced a gig at the Sunflower Lounge for the same date, and things were looking up.

Next, I found out that there was a film featuring Mike Skinner and leading light of Brumtown grime, Jaykae, premiering at the Everyman Cinema in the Mailbox. When the Villa qualified for the promotion play-offs and the crucial home leg was scheduled for the same night, it seemed like Birmingham was to be the centre of the universe on this particular Tuesday and I was suddenly spoiled for choice.

Villa solved one issue by selling out of tickets before I could do anything about it, and truth be told, the Birmingham grime documentary at the Mailbox, good as it promised to be, couldn't match the magnetic spell that an AffieJam gig casts over me. So, with my medical ordeal over with, I was in good spirits as I settled down outside the Sunny with a packet of fags and a pint of Rekorderlig cider.

I usually press gang a few friends and family into attending gigs with me, but although her bank manager won't thank me for it, I don't drag anyone along to AffieJam performances, for the simple reason that I can't stand anyone talking to me when she's on. So, feeling a bit lonely, I got chatting to a couple of blokes sharing my table outside – one of whom runs the IndieMidlands website, the other was a fellow reviewer – and after convincing them that Peace are the best band in the world at the moment – FACT – I go on to wax even more lyrical about tonight's act. 'She does everything – she's a singer, songwriter, multi-instrumentalist, hair-braider, writes wonderful prose and enlightening serious articles, blogs, illustrates, crafts … you name it, she does it.'

My glowing testimonial is interrupted rather abruptly as the singer herself comes outside to say a quick hello minutes before going on stage, and my two new acquaintances are stunned into silence. As she goes back into the venue, one of them says, 'Wow, how can you talk about her for five minutes without mentioning how beautiful she is?' The answer is that there's a lot else to talk about, but hey, if it gets their attention.

Affie opens with her well established and popular cover of Nirvana's 'Smells Like Teen Spirit', which I have grown to love despite not being a huge fan of the original. Something about the melancholic way she performs it, her luxurious voice accompanied only by her own intricate finger-picking on electric guitar, seems more appropriate for the song's subject matter than the Seattle band's raucous delivery. She follows this up with 'Are you not Satisfied?', a new song about the fragility of the artist, a gentle reminder that although we may put them on a pedestal, they are only human like the rest of us, sharing the same stresses and strains. It also touches on the strange relationship between star and audience and the way we consume art.

The next number is 'Control', and the opening line – 'Got me hanging on your every word' – could just as easily be the enrapt audience emoting to Affie as the other way round. A vibrant cover of the Noisettes' (whatever happened to them?) 'Don't Upset the Rhythm' features some enthusiastic call-and-response vocals with the crowd, led by Affie's trusted collaborator Jabez Walsh, who seems to be having a night off and is amongst the ranks of the Affie-cionados (we're like Justin's Beliebers, only less hysterical and more discerning).

We are then treated to one of our girl's most popular tunes, the stunningly beautiful and folky 'Put Aside'. This is the first song of hers I ever heard, the bright light that led me to her distant shore, and I never tire of hearing it. Her voice on it is understated yet powerful, with added weight from some gorgeous lyrics – 'I cannot be bound/cuz in you I have found/my release'.

The next song is a real plea from the heart. 'Take Me Away,' she implores, with a vocal as clear as a bell, and by this time I'm so emotionally engaged I only just resist the temptation to book us a couple of flights on my phone. The show closes with Little Dragon cover 'Twice', for which Jabez joins her on stage to add perfect harmonies. It was a breathtaking performance, and at times I was close to tears with the sheer beauty of it all.

There's a short list of artists who can tempt me away from Villa Park on a night like tonight, and AffieJam is right at the top of it. She'd better not have a gig on the day of the final.

YIKES!

Birmingham-based anti-pop quartet Y!KES (starring TJ Weston on drums, Matt Ford on bass, Liam Howard on guitar and the voice of Oli Long) released their single 'Pirouette' in the summer of 2020, accompanied by a new music video. The single was the first from their EP *Mass!ve*, which has since been on heavy rotation at Pennell Towers – 'heavy' being the operative word. I saw them live at Mama Roux's pre-lockdown and was blown away. I could tell from the new single, with an opening salvo that reminded me of the Sex Pistols' 'Holidays in the Sun', that the band are not messing about. But if anything, things get even better from then on.

'Alice' and 'Door Frame Angel' shouldn't be listened to after dark, lest they summon up the devil, while 'Faker' and EP closer 'Step Away' are reminiscent of early Oasis at their very best, the latter especially sounding deliciously radio ready. I caught up with frontman Oli Long to investigate further.

Fill me in on the history of Y!KES. The driver-turned-lead-singer story sounds interesting:

Yeah, that's pretty much how it started for me. I saw them post on Facebook looking for someone to drive their gear. I replied to it, they must have thought I was pretty cool or something because I was asked to play lead guitar after a short while. But I was pretty bad, so I guess nothing happened until I was singing 'Lithium' by Nirvana while me and Liam were driving up to a gig. I remember Liam turning to me and saying something along the lines of 'that was cool', and before I knew it, I was having a mini X-Factor audition at his house, at which he said I manifested into a magnificent eagle like from Stepbrothers, so it was a 'yes' from him and the rest is history.

So I can put Nirvana down as an influence then? Who else? I got New York Dolls and Stooges vibes when I saw you live.

Yeah, Nirvana are definitely an influence, and The Stooges of course, Iggy Pop is mega. But also Bowie, Michael Jackson, The Beatles, Oasis, Queen, Radiohead, Jeff Buckley, U2, Alice In Chains, The Prodigy – a pretty broad spectrum to be honest.

I love the 'Hold on to Your Grudge' video. What's the story behind that one?

That was our first video together. We managed to hijack a church (literally) and we put together something pretty cool. I can't remember what it was supposed to really signify, but there's some funny skitz in a pub with some garlic bread. I lost my voice due to the first scene where I was in the bath smoking fags, because as the camera is turning at the start, I had to be in the bath by the time he had made the turn, so it gave the effect of me having no reflection, but as these things go, I had to do it twenty times and blew my throat up. Other than that, it's a decent tune, but our newer stuff is getting more where it needs to be.

So you feel you've progressed from your earlier stuff? What have you learned or improved upon?

There's more of a fusion now. I've been allowed to bring my side into it a bit more with the new one and any project in the future. I come from a drum-and-bass sort of production, so there's loads more ear candy and tricks in the production process. But just in general, mine and Liam's ability to write a song together is pretty mind bending, feels almost like forces out of our control. But I've actually developed somewhat of a voice now which helps I guess … rather than relentless shouting I seem to have gained some control and composure. It just makes the tracks sound more 'professional', whatever that means.

The first time I met Liam he just seemed to manifest in the shadows of Lower Trinity Street, like there was something of the night about him. How would you describe him and what do you think he'd say about you?

Definitely, he's a shadowy spectre for sure. I'd describe him in an almost biblical fashion, Jesus-like properties, or the above to my below, or the yin to my yang. It's strange for me to have met somebody so similar but sculpted by very different hands. Then to be able to sit in a room together and make music is just weird. But I always feel like we were going to be forced together at some stage in life, whether we liked it or not. I don't know what he would say about me, and he knows I don't really care.

Have you led him astray?

Yes, but this path is pretty exciting to stumble across when you know what way you're going.

Sounds wild. Is there anyone in the band who when they walk in, the fun stops? Like, stop playing with the dynamite now Oli, time to sound check or tune up?

No not really, it seems fairly contradictory when we're all holding a stick of dynamite.

Which local band or artist are you mates with, who are your tips for the top, and who do you have a crush on?

I've personally got a lot of time for an artist called Veda. Love his imagery, the tunes are edgy & pure. And The Pagans S.O.H., who bring some real psychedelic vibes wrapped up in some kind of gunslinging rap burrito. Also there's another band who I really enjoy called Marstone, who resurrect some of my idols from the 90s in their song writing and imagery. I couldn't give a tip for the top though really, because it doesn't actually boil down to who or what I like or think, but how hard the band or artist are willing to work for it, the team of people they have around them if they're lucky, the vision and of course the tunes. All of that needs to be there, if by the top, you're talking the next Beatles. I have a crush on my girlfriend, who is gorgeousity made flesh.

Finally, what are your thoughts on the new EP?

I think the EP speaks for itself, in the music and obviously the title. I guess it's our compressed version of Nevermind.

SONIC BOOM IN B-TOWN

My mate Jason Donnelly comes from half the world away to witness the best of Brum in Balsall Heath ...

SONIC GUN WEEKENDER @ THE CASTLE AND FALCON, BALSALL HEATH

The number one showcase for Birmingham indie music, the second annual Sonic Gun Weekender, took place at the Castle and Falcon last weekend. I've heard the venue address given as Moseley before now, but if I lived in Balsall Heath I'd probably say Moseley as well – cheaper insurance and more tempting for gig-goers who are not that keen on taking a walk on the wild side. The area has been cleaned up by the residents recently, though, and its once-questionable reputation is now more folklore than fact.

The beautifully curated line-up reads like a directory of #madlands, the soubriquet often given to the burgeoning indie scene currently centred on Birmingham, and was enough to tempt my mate over from New Zealand for the weekend. He's been radicalised by the videos and streams I've been bombarding him with from the other side of the world via the internet, and I was confident that by the end of proceedings, he would feel that his journey, from where they filmed *Lord of the Rings* to the city that inspired it, was worthwhile. It must have sounded a bit dodgy as I introduced him to everybody as 'a bloke I met on the internet', but what the hell, it's 2019.

Out of the three of us who were going, the two from Henley-in-Arden and Chelmsley Wood were late, while the guy who travelled from NZ was on time, meaning we missed a fair few of the acts, but we managed to see most of our favourites, starting with Karkosa on Friday night. Half an hour flew by as they skipped through their set, made up of upbeat tunes with choruses as bouncy as the young crowd moshing in front of them.

Their already massive sound (two guitars, keyboards, drums and a new bass player) was augmented by, of all things, a trumpet. It worked perfectly, although the five-pronged attack lined up across the width of the stage was a tight squeeze. Catchy singles 'Mango Tree', 'Aurora' and the brilliant, Fratellis-like 'Red Hoodie' went down a storm – it was just a pity that their set was cut short due to time pressures before we had a chance to sing along to their anthem 'Sheffield'.

If I had to sum up their set, or indeed their whole vibe, in one word, it would be 'joyful'. No wonder parts of South Korea have fallen completely under their spell.

After appearing way down the bill at last year's event, it was a sign of the rapid rise of The Clause that they closed the first night this year – and what a finale they provided. 'Tokyo', with its spoken-word intro over a hypnotic rhythm and riff, is the perfect curtain raiser and the shape of things to come. I have to be honest and admit that I wasn't keen on next single, 'Hate the Player', at first, but it's growing on me with every listen, and the hint of Neil Young's 'Ohio' I hear in the riff makes it a worthy addition to the six bona-fide classics they've released so far.

Talking of classics, 'Cigarette Kiss' could be another one if maybe there was an extra verse and a bridge, and 'Comedown Conversations' already is. 'Dig this Beat' has the kind of chorus that's so good you think you've heard it dozens of times before, by the Arctic Monkeys, or was it the Libertines? I dunno, someone who's got post-punk guitar pop totally sussed, anyway. I'm not a fan of the slow-down/speed-up bit in the middle, but only because I think such a great song doesn't need a gimmick.

'Sixteen' sounds like something Paul Weller might have written in his Jam days and would have slotted in nicely between 'Saturday's Kids' and 'Eton Rifles' on the *Setting Sons* album. Totemic ballad 'Where are you Now?' stills the crowd into a state of reverential awe and sparks the realisation that these guys are writing teenage anthems while they are still actual teenagers.

'Shut Me Out' boasts emotionally mature lyrics beyond their years and for a moment I thought the song's visceral power had closed the show. Then I remembered that they hadn't played 'In my Element' yet and they HAD to, didn't they?

Sure enough, frontman Pearce introduced it with the question, 'Who wants to hear a top fifty single then?' Modesty must have forbade him from mentioning that it reached top spot in the iTunes Rock Chart, but what a fantastic end to a thrilling performance. I tweeted a while ago that they are the most exciting band in Britain and as I relived the gig on the way home, I was even more convinced.

The three somewhat hungover survivors from Friday (me, Jason and Simon Pitt from the Birmingham Music Awards) were joined by my wife Kerri for part two on Saturday, and we made it a bit earlier this time. The first band we saw were Spilt Milk Society, bringing their beautifully crafted song-writing skills and accomplished musicianship to the party. They really are a fantastic band to listen to at home, in the car or on your headphones, and their songs 'Amsterdam', 'Brunch' and 'She Tastes Like Summer' are three of the best I've heard from any of the Madlands groups.

However, for some reason they seemed to leave out their up-tempo numbers and crowd pleasers – maybe not the wisest policy in front of a big crowd. Spilly Milk are on a par with the all the other great local bands, but I feel they missed a chance to prove it when leaving out the likes of the brilliant 'Turtleneck Boy'. They must have their reasons I suppose – all I know is that if my band had ever written anything anywhere near as good, we'd still be touring now, thirty years after we split up over being utterly sh … I mean … musical differences.

I tempted Wifey into coming by informing her The Novus were on – after seeing them live the other month, she became as big a fan as I am. Needless to say, they didn't disappoint, but I'm seeing them again at their own headline show next month and I've got a feeling I'm going to need all the superlatives I can muster for that one. Well, okay, maybe I can spare you one word – electrifying.

They were followed by the wonderwall of psychedelic hair and guitars served up by Lichfield's Violet, another band who I suspect are destined for greatness. Check out the beautifully melodic and ethereal 'Heaven Adores You' and stone-cold banger 'Feel' and I'm sure you'll agree.

Sugarthief, joined on keyboards by Spilt Milk main man Harry, brought down the curtain on the weekend with a set list that showcased their verve and versatility. Old school White-Stripey rockers like 'When did it all go so Wrong?' were interspersed with the Pink Floyd vibes of their newer, subtler songs 'Good Luck', 'I Hope you Make it', 'Talk in Moderation' and 'Modern Man'. There was sadly no room for my personal favourite, their tribute to Brum's best merchandise shop, 'Provide', but they finished, as they kind of had to, with the epic, yearning power ballad that is 'Joy Affair'. As always, it brought the house down.

It was a superb set, and a fitting ending that impressed my Kiwi mate enough to ensure that a bit of their merch is being sported in New Zealand as I type. The standard of the current Birmingham indie scene is incredibly high and threatens to eclipse some of the giants of the genre that have gone before. As Toyah Wilcox might have said, it's a mystery to me that when being interviewed on Radio One the other week, B-Town trailblazers Swim Deep were somewhat reluctant to big up the Brum music scene and volunteer names of the many artists aiming to break into the mainstream.

Surely it wouldn't hurt to shout out the local bands, including Sugarthief, who supported them at their recent comeback residency at the Sunflower? Or even their own brothers-in-arms JAWS, who released a great album this year and whose lead singer Connor DJ'd for them at one of the shows? Let's have it right, I love Swim Deep – my recent review is testament to that. But I thought their reticence in supporting their fellow Brummie bands was a bit remiss of them. Perhaps, given the explosion in new local talent, the King City icons think their crown is slipping.

GRINDING OUT A RESULT

Like a football anorak in the 92 Club obsessing over visiting every single league club's ground, I like to get round Birmingham's legendary music venues as often as the life of a shift worker will allow, and I've ticked most of them off already. I was a bit too young to see Pink Floyd record half of the *Ummagumma* album at Mothers in Erdington, or Black Sabbath invent heavy metal at the Crown on Station Street, but I did see the Jam at Barbarellas and Dexy's at the Rum Runner (okay, they were there on a night out rather than playing live, but it still counts). I've also seen Lady Sanity at the Night Owl, Lady Sanity at the Flapper, Lady Sanity at Suki10c, Lady Sanity at the Hare and Hounds, and Lady Sanity at the Sunflower; in fact, if Lady Sanity was on in a working men's club in Carlisle on a Tuesday dinnertime, I'd do my best to get there – whereas if Coldplay were playing in my back garden I'd draw the curtains.

So, the prospect of the Queen of Brumtown hip-hop just a bus ride away in such an iconic venue as the Town Hall was irresistible to me, and it was her name on the poster that sold me the ticket. And I'm glad it did, because there was so much more to discover on the rest of an extensive bill …

THE GRIND LIVE @ BIRMINGHAM TOWN HALL, APRIL 2019

The Grind Live is a yearly showcase of the best in local soul, hip-hop, RnB, grime and spoken word, and the show was opened by Casey Bailey, who performed a beautiful poem, completely unaccompanied and all the more moving for that. Then it was Sanity time, purposefully positioned early in the night to ensure a healthy and enthusiastic crowd from the off. Resplendent in a Beat Girl dress and headscarf (an emotional reminder for me of the recently departed Ranking Roger), she laid down probably the best lyrics heard at this venue since Charles Dickens read from *A Christmas Carol* here in 1853. I was thinking more of *Oliver Twist* when she went off after two songs ('Please sir, I want some more'), but overall, I was happy to hear one new banger, 'Beauty in the Struggle', and established favourite 'Firin''.

Infamous Dimez and his sensual, smooth RnB was next, and he's definitely one to watch, although his final song probably comes with a parental guidance warning. A live cypher, performed by volunteers from the crowd as well as tonight's compère, Vital, hinted at the amazing pool of talented MCs in Birmingham. The competition in the city is so strong it's hellishly difficult to stand out, which is probably why the rappers who do (Leshurr, Sanity, Jaykae, Mist, Truemendous) are so damn good. That said, Kingstanding boy, Mayday, and Vital absolutely shut down the show with their improvised bars, before getting into some light-hearted banter over Mayday's pro-Birmingham speech, with Wolverhampton's Vital responding with, 'Can we say West Midlands?'

The Town Hall has hosted premieres of works by Felix Mendelssohn and Edward Elgar, but it's a fair bet that it has never seen the like of the next act, Tanya Cracknell, aka 'The Grime Violinist'. Classically trained, she now uses her finely honed skills to add grace and melody to 140 BPM bangers. Not classical, but still class.

By this time, I'd been celebrating picking the winner in the Grand National a bit too heavily to take notes – I spent most of my winnings on Old Mout Cider – but I do recall that P Shand and C4 (brother of legendary UK garage producer, Preditah) elicited a pretty wild response from the crowd. The presence of a few dozen Erdington goons ensured that things got even wilder when headliner Yatez took the stage.

The 24-year-old rapper-cum-RnB-singer is north Birmingham's answer to Jaykae, who he supported towards the end of last year at the Small Heath MC's massive hometown show at the Institute. Big trainers to fill, but he didn't put a foot wrong on Saturday.

Opening number 'Moving On' immediately had the audience singing along, and even the people I was with who'd never heard him before were impressed. 'Falling' is another one with a big chorus, and this merged into the brilliant 'Top Striker', his latest release. 'Do for your Love' showcased Yatez' talent for melody and high-speed rapping dexterity, as well as the beautiful voice of Chelsea on backing vocals.

There was only one way to finish – with the obviously heartfelt tribute to a city, 'Birmingham Crew' – 'We could end up in paradise/but this will always be my home'. A fitting end to the evening, as we were already (literally and figuratively) in Paradise. The decision, back in the 1830s, to build the Town Hall in Paradise Street instead of Bennetts Hill had never made more sense.

The night ended on a personal high when a very well refreshed and friendly gay man said I was 'quite nice looking' and propositioned me on the bus home. As a deliriously happily married man, I politely declined.

INTRODUCING ...
SPILT MILK SOCIETY

Writing about music is not all champagne and supernovas – this was the second of two gigs on consecutive nights, and after both of them I had to be up at four in the morning. Wifey had looked after the kids, so fair's fair, it's her turn to go out on Saturday.

Staying in with the remote to myself has its compensations, though, *Match of the Day* and *The Rap Game UK* amongst them, but the highlight of any Saturday evening at home for me is the BBC WM *Introducing* show at 8 p.m. – essential listening that keeps me up to date with the new music on the scene that I haven't got time to investigate for myself.

I first stumbled across the programme back in the Louise Brierley/Jack Parker era, since when Louise has moved on and Jacky P has run off with Scarlord on a seemingly endless tour, taking hardcore Brummie rock-rap to the world. Now the inestimable Alex Noble is at the controls, and for two informative hours every week he, Tim Senna, Harry Bozman and producer Thea Matthews do a great job of promoting new West Midlands music, through interviews, reports and erm ... playing the songs, obvs – both official releases and those sent in by aspiring artists to the BBC WM uploader. They've opened my ears to literally dozens of artists who I now love – and long may it continue. Alex is keen to make the show an even bigger part of the scene and, partnering with Birmingham Promoters and the Castle and Falcon, he puts on an occasional showcase of leading local acts. The first featured Ivory Wave and Karkosa, and tonight is part two of what will hopefully turn into a long-running series.

SPILT MILK SOCIETY, CAGE PARK, THE VERSE @ THE CASTLE AND FALCON

I arrived halfway through the The Verse's set and was impressed by the bit I witnessed. I've seen them perform a couple of songs on *Raw Sound TV* but experiencing them in the flesh made a bigger dent in my consciousness. They were tight, accomplished and dynamic, and from talking to others it seemed they made quite an impact. Their occasional three-part harmonies are on point and something you don't see enough of these days.

Cage Park are a band I've been wanting to see for ages – actually, it can't be ages because they haven't been alive that long – but gigs clashing with family occasions and other logistical problems have conspired to keep us apart until now. As they took the stage, I was grateful it was a 14+ show or they wouldn't have got in, and although I've put away a couple of ciders already, the realisation that their combined age was only just above my individual one was a sobering thought. To be fair though, their age shouldn't come into it – it's just easy to write about – and I'd still be reporting that they are freakishly talented even if they were in their mid-twenties.

Opening number 'Tunnel Vision' is like something off Peace's *Delicious* EP but remixed by Kurt Cobain. Second song 'Keep It' sounds like XTC or Gang of Four and wouldn't be out of place on Paul Weller's finest hour as a songwriter, The Jam's *Sound Affects*.

Their versatility is highlighted as Edie seamlessly takes on front-woman duties while Arthur plays Edie's bass like a natural; Leo, an enormous influence on the overall sound, plays the ultimate guitar hero as another local musician incredulously shouts down my ear, informing me that he hasn't left Year 10 yet.

All this while Reuben, a dead ringer for Jack Webster off *Coronation Street*, looks like he's having the time of his life on drums. I don't think he stopped smiling throughout, and why should he? His bandmates reckon he's the best drummer in Birmingham and there's absolutely no doubt he's in one of the city's – scratch that, the nation's – most promising groups. On latest single 'Lightning', he stands up behind the kit to lead handclaps and the crowd enthusiastically join in, and you're left wondering how the hell these youngsters have completely mastered the art of writing indie-punk bangers and made them as catchy as the *Happy Days* theme tune.

They finish with 'Castle of Cards' and I'm contemplating if this was what it was like watching the Arctic Monkeys before they were famous. Cage Park's parents must have an awesome record collection, although I suspect the Childish Gambino reference in the lyrics is all the band's own work.

After their set, I totally fan-boy Arthur and he helps me with the few lines of lyrics from 'Lightning' that I couldn't quite make out. Fair play to them for not once taking the easy option and rhyming it with 'frightening'.

It's a hard act to follow, and it's weird to type, but Spilt Milk Society handle it like the seasoned veterans that, compared to Cage Park, they are. They open with the gorgeous 'She Tastes Like Summer', Harry's powerful voice resonating throughout the 300-capacity room.

They're a band of many talents, and all are on show during record of the year contender 'Turtleneck Boy', an indie-pop masterpiece, followed by the 'Bohemian Rhapsody' of B-Town, the epic 'Brunch'. It's a beautiful song that boasts power and vulnerability in equal measure, and leads into a storming 'Cops and Robbers', which is about as vulnerable as the Peaky Blinders. Harry breaks a string on the power chords that run through the song and has to appeal to the previous acts to borrow a new one for the finale, 'Amsterdam', during which Cage Park are amongst the most excited kids in the chaotic mosh pit. As the sweaty, satisfied crowd disperses, I spy Alex Noble from BBC WM *Introducing* looking justifiably pleased with himself. It was a great show and a triumph for Alex and his team. I congratulate him and ask him about the ethos of these events:

I think it's so important that our programme is a big part of the music scene here in the West Midlands but not just on the airwaves. Since I've come into this role, I've made it a big mission to do more work in the live community here and this showcase is the perfect example of how the programme can be helpful in more ways than just airplay.

I tell him it's working, and that Tim Senna is the embodiment of the show's presence at gigs.

'That's really good to hear,' he replies. 'We've worked really hard on being that force for good – it helps that the scene is the way it is right now – and Tim is a blessing to have on board.'

Tim hasn't been at the last two gigs I've been to – I've since found out he's on holiday – but he's usually so omnipresent that his absence makes you think you're in a different city. He, Alex and the rest of their team, along with their connections to the rest of the BBC radio network, are fast becoming a huge asset to the local music scene. BBC Music *Introducing* in the West Midlands airs every Saturday night from 8 p.m. on BBC WM 95.6 and you can listen again on the BBC Sounds App.

NORTHERN EXPOSURE

North Parade have been causing quite a stir on local radio for a while now, with a handful of individually released indie bangers peppering the airwaves. Their first release was a song called 'Birmingham' – I was immediately intrigued by the title alone – and they've retained my interest with their debut EP, *How to be Good*. The intrigue starts with the opening bars of 'The NOW', and the quality never dips with the jaunty, angular pop of 'Keep Things Casual', the sublime 'Someone' and the epic scale of 'An Accommodation'. I spoke to lead singer Henry Plumridge to find out more.

The band are from all over the country — how come you're considered a Birmingham band?

I think we identify with Birmingham the most because it's where we all met. It's also where we first started practising and playing. Despite being from all over, when we return to Birmingham it's always a nice feeling. And no rehearsal space ever has matched Muthers!

I suppose having a song called 'Birmingham' helps. The city is not referenced in the lyrics, so what's the story behind the title?

People always seem to pick up on this, which is funny because when I wrote it I didn't think too much about it. It just seemed to fit. It was written at a time in my life where I was between places a lot. I think I've mentioned this before, but I actually wrote the lyrics at a motorway services between Birmingham and Oxford. The lyrics are all very literal, so it made sense to have a direct and literal title too. As well as that, I quite liked the idea that there were millions of songs referencing 'Paris' or 'New York' and that I could make that little trope my own.

I first saw you live supporting Karkosa. Are you mates with them? Who else do you rate?

Karkosa are great. We've played with them lots and I'd say we know them pretty well now. That night particularly, they were great, I thought – a really varied and polished set. There are a lot of other good Birmingham bands too: Riscas, Sugarthief and Ivory Wave all come to mind. We've never played with any of them but hope to have the chance to one day.

Why do you take your shoes off to play live?

This was actually originally just because I had a very small button on a pedal that I needed to press, and I couldn't do it with shoes on. But it always got people talking for some reason so even when that pedal went, I kept the shoes off. I actually much prefer playing like it, not sure why.

I first heard you through Tim Senna's recommendation. He's a great advocate of the local scene, so it must be nice to have him championing you.

Tim's been so supportive right from the start. He's got an infectious enthusiasm for Birmingham and all new indie music and so to have him on our side is amazing. I've also got to know him personally quite well and he's offered lots of good advice and is generally just a lovely guy.

'An Accommodation' is one of your best tunes and shares a title with a poem by Simon Armitage. Any connection?

Yeah, it was a very conscious decision to name it after that poem. The lyrics also make use of the same double meaning that the poem does; an accommodation, like a place to stay, and also 'accommodating' someone. I always found the poem to be really beautiful and loved the title for years. It was just a case of waiting for the right time to use it really.

Who are the other guys in the band, and how did it all begin?

I posted on a Facebook page, actually, the first day I started at Birmingham University, saying something along the lines of 'does anyone want to play some music with me?' Ollie, the drummer, replied fairly quickly and we met for a drink. Ollie had already met James, the bass player, at a house party I think, and so we met with him to ask if he wanted to play with us and he said yes. Since then we've undergone a few personnel changes on lead guitar. At the moment Tom Alford plays with us, who's a friend I know from back home in Oxford. Oh, and I play guitar, occasional harmonica and sing.

Is there a song by someone else you wish you'd written?

If I'm honest, barely a day of listening to music goes by without me thinking, 'Damn I wish I'd written that'. I always say the two songs I'm most in awe of ever are 'Visions of Johanna' by Bob Dylan and 'There is a Light that Never Goes Out' by The Smiths. If I am ever able to write a song with a tenth of the beauty those songs have, I'll be immensely pleased with myself. As well as them, the song I most recently thought this about was 'Can't Take My Eyes Off You' by Franki Valli. The chords meander through all sorts of interesting changes but the hooks are so clear and immediate, it's genius.

On a similar theme, how about a line-up for a fantasy supergroup with you as lead singer?

Goodness. I've never thought about this. I'd have John Densmore on drums – I can't listen to the Doors without thinking how great he is. I'd be foolish to not have Paul McCartney on bass. Johnny Marr would have to be the guitarist. And just so I get to play with him, I'd have Bob Dylan switching between acoustic guitar and keyboards. Ideally, he could also write the lyrics.

High standards indeed, and on their debut EP, North Parade have set some pretty high ones of their own.

TWO WORLDS COLLIDE

Birmingham has a long history and tradition of musical innovation, and at the dawn of a new decade the Brummies are at it again. All across the city's urban recording studios, producers and engineers are pushing boundaries; MCs with fresh flows are riding new rhythms and beats; cultures are clashing and collaborating, creating shards of gritty, grimy glass that are set to pierce the zeitgeist. And now the city that kept grime alive while others pronounced it dead is about to breathe new life into UK rap yet again.

Leading the revolution is Screama, the renowned Birmingham producer, who joined forces with Daniel Sturridge's Dudley Road Records label for their first release, and counts the likes of Safone, George the Poet, Trilla Jermaine Trilloski and Knox Brown amongst his many production credits. He has worked on several Ministry Of Sound compilations and, alongside Papez Musix, founded The HitMonsterz, an eight-strong crew of producers whose credits include Aystar, Giggs, Ashanti, Wiley, Lady Leshurr, Bowzer Boss, Anderson 100 and more.

With over 100 unreleased songs on file, and 680,000 Spotify streams to his name, covering the bases of trap, rap, grime, garage, bassline and Latin, you could say that Screama is fluent in the international language of music. And 2020 sees his journey take another turn as he links up with highly rated US rapper, Allwinsnoloss.

The Baltimore-raised MC came up in a strict military household, with not much of a social life and few friends, and had a lot of responsibilities throughout his teenage years. It felt as though he was forced to grow up early and missed out on being a kid, with everything around shaping him into something he didn't want to be. Because of the pressures he faced from the environment around him and conflicts with his father, AWOL struggled to express himself, and it wasn't until he went off to college in Atlanta and attended an open-mic night on campus that he discovered his words resonated with people his own age.

Eventually, he was introduced to big-time producer and rapper Sonny Digital and there followed a session at Sonny's home studio, where he recorded his first-ever track. AWOL dropped his debut mixtape, *For Smokers Only*, in 2018. I caught up with AWOL and Screama to talk in more detail about their collaboration … and lots of other stuff besides.

George Bernard Shaw said that the US and Britain are two countries separated by a common language. That's certainly true in rap, where the UK has developed its own distinct style and flow. What were the challenges of making beats for an American MC?

Screama: For me there was no real challenge here because I have been making UK and American music for years, just through being a fan and an appreciator of music. I've ended up dabbling in a lot of current sounds which made me more than prepared for this opportunity.

Are your lyrics very different to homegrown MCs, and how closely do you think British audiences will relate to them?

AWOL: They are different for sure because of life experience, etc., but I wouldn't say they are miles off what current UK artists are speaking about. The landscape here has changed, and you can see that when you look at groups like DBE. The lines have been blurring between UK and USA music.

What led to you moving to the UK?

AWOL: My whole life I felt like I didn't belong in my country. In my home, I was taught to be proud of my culture, to love my family, and was told that I could do anything. In school I was taught 'one nation under God with liberty and justice for all'.

The American system teaches equality and is founded on the principles of Christianity and to love one another as we love ourselves. But I see a people who hate themselves, not because they are incapable of showing love, but because they are conditioned to, so therefore they show hate to others. I see the devilish frown in the form of racism, inequality, hypocrisy, white supremacy and slavery disguised as politics on the face of a country who hides behind a mask with a smile, dressed up in the core values that the country is said to represent.

I've never had a culture, I've never been treated as an equal, I've always been judged and stereotyped and negatively depicted to be something I'm not – or even negatively depicted to be something I am – as a direct result of the system that is in place in my country.

Honestly, I just got tired of all the lies, negativity, crabs in a barrel mentality, and superficial mindset that comes with being in America. I knew it was time to leave when I saw the finalists of the 2016 presidential election. And more so when I saw the racist/ racially insensitive/racial indifference of both candidates. I love being an American, I just wish we would do better.

Do you like the UK any better?

AWOL: I can't say that I do like it, but I can't say that I don't like it either. Home is home, so nothing is gonna be as fun and heart-warming as that. But at the same time, I like how open minded the United Kingdom is and I love the culture here. People here aren't as uptight and enjoy the little things. Plus, the police don't carry guns so I'm not worried about losing my life just because somebody on a power trip with a badge doesn't like how I carry myself.

How did the two of you link up?

Screama: We met when Trilla Jermaine Trilloski and I flew out to Ibiza. We were in a club vibing out and AWOL had lost his friends …
AWOL: I saw another guy with dreads [Screama] in the crowd and Trilla with his braids and thought 'Imma go and roll with these guys'. I went over and invited them both to bottles at the bar. At the end of the night we went our own way, but in the airport we found each other again, discovered we all make music and I told them I lived in the UK, so we exchanged details.
Screama: Two weeks later, AWOL did an all-weekender in the studio with myself, Trilla, SG [Bassline artist] and guests such as DJ Biggoss & KE4T, where I made beats from scratch and AWOL recorded at least eight full tracks in the first night alone.

When will we hear the fruits of the collab?

Screama: It's already started in January with 'Shanghai' being released, and through-out 2020 we will release the fire.

Where do you think Birmingham stands in relation to other UK cities in terms of the urban music being produced here?

Screama: I think some of the best, most innovative music is produced here and has been for a very long time. It's just now finally getting some light shed on it. So watch this space! If the city lacks anything at all, it's that we could have more people who want to work in music from a management/PR/marketing aspect. Not everyone needs to be on the stage!

What you're doing here seems quite pioneering. Do you think this US/UK cross-pollination will grow in the future?

Screama: 1,000%! These things take time, but that's because you can't rush greatness. Once the path has been set and laid out there will be no going back, so I'm just happy and grateful to be a part of the merging of worlds!

KERRI STEALS THE SHOW

If you've paid attention up to now, you'll understand why there are few menus in music more appetising to me than Namywa playing at Mama Roux's while Digbeth Dining Club is in full swing outside, and it's a prospect that me, two of my kids and a couple of my wife Kerri's cousins, who came up from London especially, couldn't resist.

I arrived early because I didn't want to miss a beat, and it wasn't difficult to spot Namz in the crowded venue, looking fabulous in a jumpsuit of sequins and sparkles as she chatted to fans. Her shows come with a cast-iron guarantee of quality, and any surprises arise only from the fact that one never knows exactly how she will deliver on that promise. Sometimes backed by a nine-piece band, as was the case last time I saw her at the Hare and Hounds, sometimes, like tonight, a more intimate affair, comprising Rachel and Sadie on backing vocals, Ian Silk on acoustic guitar and the irrepressible and stylish Glyn Phillips on percussion.

Namywa opens with the funky groove of 'Wound Up', one of my wife's favourite tunes, so she'll be gutted that she's … erm, … 'stranded' in a swanky cocktail bar across town, celebrating landing a new job. First-world problems or what?

The strident 'Let Me Treat You Right' is next, before Namywa offers a rare glimpse of touching vulnerability on 'Stupid Me', a moving account of falling in love with a friend. She dedicates joyful love song 'Only the Sweetest' to a happy couple in front of the stage celebrating their wedding anniversary, and the show couldn't have been going any better.

Then things got messy. During the quiet introduction to 'F*** the Media' (a calm before the storm if ever there was one), a stunningly attractive young woman in heels tottered up to the front of the stage, obviously as well refreshed as anybody else in Digbeth on a Saturday night, and loudly expressed her pleasure at seeing her cousins, her stepsons and her husband – me. Over an hour before, she had vaguely promised that she was just finishing her current drink and making her way over, but due to an incredible stroke of bad luck, had managed to find the only taxi driver in town who didn't know where Digbeth Dining Club was.

You know what incredible means, right? Displaying admirable professional- ism, Namywa held off on the vocals until Kerri had finished her salutations – I think Ian played the intro another twice – and she must have been wondering, 'How many times has this girl got to say hello?'

About a minute later, calm was finally restored – briefly – and then Namywa let rip with the scorching lyrics, eviscerating branches of the media that frequent- ly exploit women in their portrayal of them. Kerri would have been raising her fist in solidarity had she known what day it was.

Now I had an unruly spouse to look after, I'm afraid my set-list notes went for a burton, but I'm pretty sure we were treated to the gorgeous 'Summer's Night in June' and the uncompromising 'Get to Know Me Again' before the interval, perfectly timed for those who wanted to partake in the delights of the street food on offer, or maybe, hopefully, PLEASE, just sober up a bit, for pity's sake.

NAMYWA. (© LEE CRAWFORD, DISTORTED IMAGE PHOTOGRAPHY)

Namywa returned to the stage with a storming cover of Eminem's 'Lose Yourself', Afrotwang banger 'Namaste', and the full-fat funk of 'Matter of Fact' to finish. I had taken a seat next to my wife after the interval and experimented with taking on the role of an impartial observer instead of a fan. As such, it was fascinating to watch an audience who had previously been unfamiliar with her work gradually but fully won over. Infectious tunes, evocative words and melodies and the sheer vibrancy of Namywa's voice and personality will do that to an audience.

The people I know in the Birmingham music industry have started to sit up and take notice in the same way, and if what I hear is true about the new songs Namywa is ready to unleash, they won't be the only ones. Expect to see, hear and read a lot more about her in future. It was quite a while ago that she promised me a seat at her table at the MOBO awards if she gets there – she can say 'if', but I'm saying 'when'.

HOMECOMING QUEEN

Stop me if you've heard this one before, but it never gets old for me. I first saw Lady Leshurr at a school concert about fifteen years ago when she dressed up as Lisa 'Left Eye' Lopes to perform TLC's 'No Scrubs' alongside my daughter Danielle and another girl (dressed as T-Boz and Chilli, I suppose). Good as I'm sure it was, I didn't remember it until my kids reminded me recently, so I very much doubt I left Archbishop Grimshaw School that night thinking little Melesha O'Garro would one day be fighting it out with Chuck D out of Public Enemy for my 'favourite ever rapper' affections.

Since then, she's clocked up 160 million YouTube views, collaborated with the likes of Stormzy, Wiley, Jaykae and will.i.am, appeared with Nicki Minaj on her recent world tour, has her own ITV show, *Don't Hate the Playaz*, and co-hosted *Later … with Jools Holland*. She's the most successful product of Kingshurst since Gary Shaw (ask yer dad), and like him, she's picked up a host of accolades, including Best Female at the MOBOs in 2016, and Best Rap/Grime Act at the 2019 Birmingham Music Awards. Now she's back on the manor doing her Citizen Leshurr bit – campaigning for the reopening of her old stamping ground, Kingshurst Youth and Community Centre (an event for the cause was recently cancelled due to concerns that too many people would turn up to see her), and tonight helping SHOUT Festival and Birmingham Open Media celebrate their birthdays.

LADY LESHURR @ BIRMINGHAM OPEN MEDIA, NOVEMBER 2019

Ten years ago, Birmingham's SHOUT Festival started from a desire to celebrate and promote the diversity of the city's LGBT cultural community – since when they've developed a dynamic annual festival, taking place for ten days every November. Meanwhile, for five years now, Birmingham Open Media has been a centre for science, technology and art, dedicated to creative innovation.

The free gallery presents cutting-edge digital artworks and exhibitions to spark debate about technology and scientific progress, with a particular interest in neurodiversity (I had to Google it), and there's a café serving organic, fair-trade coffee, tea, homemade cakes and ethically sourced food. As if that isn't recommendation enough, it's located in an area of town that should be granted World Heritage status, populated as it is by globally significant culture in the shape of the oldest working British cinema, the Electric, and the UK's first purpose-built repertory theatre, Sir Barry Jackson's Old Rep. The birthplace of heavy metal, the Crown, is on one corner of the block, and dodgy cinema Adult World is on another, causing Wifey and I to run the sticky gauntlet of middle-aged men in loose-fitting trousers as we cross Hinckley Street to the party.

We've got diversity all right, and it doesn't end there. The inclusivity of the organisations celebrating is reflected in the crowd – colourful, glamorous and fabulous in equal measure, while drag artist and host, Yshee Black, shimmers away magnificently in a sparkling blue dress and heels.

After an eclectic DJ set, Yshee gets the party started by introducing House of Bab, who treat the audience to some spectacular vogueing. Renowned DJ Sippin' T from London club night BBZ, is stuck on a rain-delayed train, but our fears about the presence of Lady Leshurr are allayed by the sight of a tray of salmon being delivered to the dressing room area. (Any of the million people who follow her on social media will know that not only does 'a salmon a day keep the battyfish away' but is also writ large and probably underlined three times on her rider.)

Sure enough, as her DJ takes over on the decks and we look around for the grime superstar, she pops up from nowhere on stage barely 6ft in front of us, dressed down in a baseball cap, sweatshirt and trackie bottoms. A surge of high-voltage electricity courses through the room as she opens with Sister Nancy's 'Bam Bam', the song she wrote her first lyrics to as a 6-year-old, which merges into a head-spinning medley including beats from Dr Dre, Rihanna and Chaka Demus and Pliers.

The Kingshurst native is visibly moved when someone shouts out her B37 postcode, before she splits the audience in two for the opening bars of 'Queen's Speech 3', which is followed by a few more of the viral freestyles that made her famous, performed in no particular order, but brilliantly, nonetheless. On 'QS5' she gets the audience jumping from side to side as if she's got us on strings, like some relentless, disciplinarian puppet-master. 'I Got the Juice' is next, followed by Leshurr showing off her melodic singing voice on the rhythmic and danceable 'On my Way'.

Other highlights include two of her latest joints, 'Black Madonna' and 'Your Mr'. Leshurr's audience engagement is inspirational as she urges others to break down barriers and follow in her footsteps and speaks of her home city being on the rise. Then, as if to prove her point, she shows support for the phenomenal crop of Brummie MCs currently making waves in The Game with shout-outs for Mist, Jaykae, Dapz On The Map, Lady Sanity and Truemendous, showing that her triumph at the Birmingham Music Awards was no walk in the park.

Sheer delirium infects the room as Leshurr takes us straight to Wakanda on her *Black Panther* freestyle, before she shuts the place down with 'the tune that bought my mum's house', 'Queen's Speech 4'. A tremendous and energetic performance, all the more remarkable as Leshurr is still grieving after the devastating recent loss of her sister Carmen to breast cancer. What a professional.

Birmingham Open Media and SHOUT couldn't have picked a better headliner for their party – a female icon, a gay icon, a Birmingham icon ... hell, let's just acknowledge she's an icon, and leave it at that.

MY SUMMER WITH THE NOVUS . . .

MAMA ROUX'S, DIGBETH; O'NEILL'S, BROAD STREET; CASTLE AND FALCON, BALSALL HEATH; QUANTUM CENTRE, DIGBETH

I first saw The Novus play live at the Birmingham Music Awards summer party at Mama Roux's, where they performed a short set that established them in a very small and exclusive club – rock bands beloved of my beloved wife. She's an avid rap and RnB fan and it takes something special to drag her kicking and screaming out of those genres and into this one – and The Novus are something special.

They're also very moreish, and within a couple of weeks of the BMAs gig I was power-walking along Broad Street on the last leg of a mad dash from work to see them again, this time at O'Neill's on Birmingham's Golden Mile. It was during the Ashes test match at Edgbaston; Broad Street was full of cricket fans from all over the country, nay world, and whilst vaping outside I made like the Harvey Keitel character in *Taxi Driver*, tempting punters by telling them of the pleasures within.

'They're like a cross between the Sex Pistols and The Clash,' I said, and the pitch seemed to work on those of a certain age. As you might expect, the attention of some of the audience was occasionally drawn to the cricket highlights that were playing on the TV screens around the bar. Over a thunderous beat, Connor, the charismatic frontman, was having none of it. He grabbed a bar stool, perched himself precariously upon it, and demanded, 'Don't watch that! I'm more important than that! WATCH MEEEEE!!' He then proceeded to wow the crowd of complete strangers with a mesmeric performance, and nobody I spoke to afterwards threatened me with the Trade Descriptions Act over my Pistols/Clash comparison.

About a month later was the Sonic Gun Weekender, and it was a sign of the lads' progress from playing last year's event at three in the afternoon that this year they were promoted up the bill to 8.30 p.m. As one of the organisers said to me a few days later, The Novus changed the whole course of the event. They drew everybody in from the beer garden on a lovely summer evening and got the place jumping. They were, for the third time I'd seen them on a multi-act bill, the best of the night, and I promised myself that wild horses wouldn't keep me away from their headline show at a secret location, finally revealed on posters around Digbeth as being at the Quantum Centre, an exhibition space in Upper Trinity Street.

Some 400 fellow Sherlocks also detected the venue, made gig-ready by the Herculean DIY efforts of the band, who built the stage and lighting rig with the help of family and friends. We sadly missed the support acts due to a combination of work, rushing round getting childcare and having to eat on the move. Still, getting our dinner from Buddha Belly at Digbeth Dining Club is never a hardship, and it certainly beats grabbing a quick Chelmsley dummy. (Chelmsley Wood is a housing estate in East Birmingham/North Solihull, where mothers who are busy shopping in the town centre are known to pacify unruly toddlers with a Greggs sausage roll – aka a 'Chelmsley dummy'.)

THE NOVUS. (© PHIL DRURY, 2324 PHOTOGRAPHY)

We entered the venue and said hello to the band's manager Andrew Winters who, unsurprisingly, I'm on speaking terms with after stalking his band round Birmingham all summer. He was once Morrissey's assistant tour manager – until the daft old racist diva sacked him for having once bought an Elton John record or something – and also used to manage B-Town legends Dodgy. So, if he's good enough for them ...

The size of the gathering was another indication of The Novus' progress: triple the number that attended their headline show at Muthers Studio earlier this year. Members of The Clause, Violet, La Dharma and Karkosa amongst them, showing just how heart-warmingly united the Birmingham scene is right now. The venue was a bit on the chilly side, a problem that was easily solved by buying a couple of T-shirts from the merch stall to wear as vests. Good marketing ploy lads!

As three-quarters of the band struck up the thrilling introduction of revolutionary call to arms 'Post-Modern Fairytale', we eagerly awaited the frontman's entrance. Would it be from stage left, stage right, from the floorboards up or from the back of the room on a zip wire? Turned out he was on stage all along, as a black cloak was pulled off a wire cage to reveal Connor, menacingly prowling around inside on all fours, singing the opening lines, 'Are you happy/In this life?' Honestly? Stood here watching the most powerful thing to come out of Birmingham since the industrial steam engine, I couldn't be happier.

'We can be the change to set you free!' he implores, with the kind of passion that makes anything seem possible, and bursts out of the cage. New songs 'Frosty', 'New Age' and 'Darkness' lead into the more familiar 'Man on the Bridge', their first song to get airplay on Radio One – a storming punk rock tribute to an old bloke who dances in his underwear at Camden Lock, like a cockney version of Bordesley Green legend Mad Malik. 'You can't tell me he's an OAP/You're having a laugh/He's got more electricity than I have.'

It's Connor who's having a laugh now – Npower hasn't got more electricity than he has. The Novus are one of the few bands on the scene these days with something worth saying about the dystopian state of the nation, and they keep the rebellious theme going with another unashamed call for civil unrest, 'Break', 'Can you feel the rumble?/Can you feel the rise?/Tell me that you're with me/ We're gonna break tonight'.

There's a costume change, from boiler suits to business suits, and we are treated to more bold, ambitious and heavier-than-the-sun rockers like 'Hate is the Cancer' and 'Castaway', on which guitarist Tom and bassist Tyla bring the beautiful noise, and Euan hits the drums harder than anyone I've ever seen. I can't wait to get familiar with the studio versions.

They know how to pick a cover too – Billie Eillish's 'Crown' is made for them. Be warned, though – they do things to it that you wouldn't do to a farmyard animal. Altogether, with Connor mixing the energy and showmanship of Johnny Rotten and Iggy Pop, they're an incredible unit, even more so when Euan's brother Harry joins the line-up to add texture with his acoustic guitar on 'Darkness', 'Moonlight' and show closer, 'Sanity'.

I had everything crossed hoping for an encore of the brilliant 'Greyscale', their first single – sadly to no avail. I've heard that the barmy a'peths don't like playing it any more. (Manager Andrew tells me that his former charges Dodgy felt the same way about 'Good Enough' until one of their dads said he liked it.) But after forty-five high-octane minutes of theatrics, crowd surfing and acrobatics, as Connor climbed up everything that WAS nailed down, I couldn't really complain.

One final surprise awaited us as we left straight after the show – Connor loitering outside, all sweaty, with make-up running down his face. He almost scared me out of my skin until I realised who he was, and he gave us a hug and thanked us for coming. An absolute showman and humble with it.

'Jesus,' I said to Wifey, as we headed into the darkness. 'He looked like Pennywise.'

'Yes bab,' she replied. 'That's the look he's going for.'

I'd be lost without her to explain things to me.

GROWING UP IN PUBLIC

The first time I saw Mahalia it might as well have been in someone's (admittedly rather large) living room. Everybody sat round her in a circle while she sang her (admittedly rather good) songs, and I could tell from the banter that I was virtually the only one there who didn't know her personally. I'd been tipped off about her by my sister-in-law Olivia, who was in her class at Birmingham Ormiston Academy, and who also warned, 'There'll be nobody there apart from her mates.' I left as a fan and hailed her as one of the West Midlands' best urban females in a now 4-year-old article.

Her progress was rapid, and in a review of a subsequent gig, I predicted that in the near future, she wouldn't have time to do the 'meet, greet, and take a selfie' thing she did at the 300-capacity Castle and Falcon, as soon she'd be playing to thousands. But I'm no Mystic Meg – by this time, her song 'Sober' on the Colours YouTube platform was turning into an unstoppable viral juggernaut, hitting 7 million views on the day of that gig. It's clocked up 40-odd million now, which goes some way to explaining the long line of fans snaking around deepest, darkest Digbeth on this cold, November night.

MAHALIA @ THE O2 INSTITUTE

The doors opened at seven, and we drove past the venue at about ten to, on our way to Digbeth Dining Club. The size of the gathering outside was alarming, but I was confident they'd be inside by the time we'd polished off our curry. No such luck. By the time we headed for the gig, the queue was past the JFK memorial mosaic and all the way down Floodgate Street. I thought I saw the end of it, but it was just another corner. One and a half streets later, we finally joined the end of the throng and from there it took us an hour to get in.

We'd booked unreserved seating on the balcony, but all the seats were occupied, and for a while it looked as though we'd be watching the show on tiptoes from behind the cast of *Land of the Giants*. Wifey doesn't do basic – she's well groomed, meticulously manicured and drives a German whip. She's got a monthly hair and nails contract, and doesn't countenance camping, glamping or standing up at gigs. When she vowed, 'Never again', it was time to get assertive with the security until they found us some comfortable seats, which they did in the nick of time, just as Mahalia appeared.

Dressed in a long, denim shirt (soon to be discarded), black leotard, fishnet tights and docs, she cut a super-confident figure as her long, braided hair followed closely behind. She opened with 'Hide Out', one of the strongest tracks on a very good debut album, *Love and Compromise*, the cover art of which adorned the stage. Straight from the kick-off, backing vocals were provided by the adoring crowd, and their harmonies were quite impressive.

As you would expect, she performed the album almost in its entirety, and I had no complaints about that. Particular highlights were 'Do Not Disturb', 'Good Company', 'Karma', 'He's Mine', dancefloor filler 'Simmer' and the beautiful, jazzy album closer, 'Square 1'. Biggest hit 'Sober' was given an appropriately big production, with a speeded-up remix tagged on at the end, and the guitar, almost a permanent fixture in her younger days, only came out for one song, 'Honeymoon'.

Wifey and I were slightly disappointed by the omission of what we both consider to be her best song, 'No Reply', but mature, accomplished ballads like 'What you Did', and the jaunty RnB pop of 'What am I?' more than made up for it. She closed the show with the brilliant 'I Wish I Missed my Ex', the final chapter in a book of malevolence towards her ex-boyfriends.

The 21-year-old writes evocatively on other relationship nuances too, but there's no denying she possesses a cutting turn of phrase when eviscerating an ex-partner, a bit like Adele but with better grooves. Long-term fans will know Mahalia doesn't do encores, but she did re-emerge to dance energetically around the stage, waving goodbye to, and feeling the love from, all corners of the delighted audience. I was cheering and clapping with the rest at such a huge and accomplished show with a great band – Ross, Dan, Samson and long-term sidekick Charlie, take a bow – but I couldn't help feeling a tinge of sadness. Her between-song patter is as witty and charming as ever, but there are fewer Birmingham stories than there used to be.

I missed the fond reminiscences of her Brummie friends, her schooldays here, and her nights at Indy Bar drinking a bottle of wine direct from the bottle through a straw. I reflected on when I used to get excited about hearing 'Silly Girl' on local radio, and then remembered how gassed I was a few months ago to hear 'Do Not Disturb' on the radio in New York. (I almost fainted when I went outside and saw her image on a huge electronic billboard in Times Square.)

Things have changed and Mahalia has grown, progressed, spread her wings and flown the nest. She's not 'ours' any more, and as a proud daughter of Leicester, maybe she never really was. She's on the road to major success and perhaps belongs to the world she's been touring, and maybe that world will one day belong to her. She'll have much better writers than me reviewing her in future, and that's a stone-cold fact.

But we should be proud of our part in the blossoming of such a huge talent, and I hope we always give her a warm welcome when she comes back to visit. As a city, we were lucky to have her, and we baked a good 'un while she was here.

MAKING WAVES

It's quite a challenge to keep up with the Birmingham music scene these days. I've already given up on the last week before Christmas – shopping and preparations dictate that I have to pick only two from Swim Deep, The New Consistent, Karkosa, The Clause, UB40, The Wonder Stuff and The Twang, meaning I have to miss six ... (SIX!) of them. And even on this seemingly insignificant November weekend, I'm spoiled for choice, as Ivory Wave and Call Me Unique pick the same night to bring their particular brands of magic to Digbeth.

Not to worry, I have the stage times and a plan.

IVORY WAVE @ THE O2 INSTITUTE

At 7.15 I'm at the O2 Institute, chatting to Ben Ramsay from The New Consistent and watching his mates, 11 57, opening the Ivory Wave show with a bang. They've been the talk of the town since their live debut at the Sonic Gun Weekender this summer, and their huge potential is hinted at as squalling lead guitar is welded onto a bluesy, heavy, early Zeppelin-style beat on 'The Way of the Bear', while their first single 'Would I Lose?' is an accomplished indie-punk party piece. They turn in a highly promising and versatile performance and look completely at home on such a huge stage for only their third gig.

As they leave, so do I, dashing round the corner hoping to catch a vibe off Call Me Unique, who is hosting her monthly show, The Unique Experience, at Mama Roux's in Lower Trinity Street. Frustratingly, she hasn't started yet, but there's time for a quick chat and a Digbeth Dining Club burger from Flying Cows on my flying visit. On the way back to the Institute, I have another pitstop at the Big Bull's Head, where DJ Steve Sainy is spinning all kinds of Northern Soul loveliness.

A few of my pals are in the house and I'm tempted to stay, but I'm intrigued by the hype surrounding Ivory Wave and, though I'm not their biggest fan, I want to give them a chance to win me over. I get back just in time to see them take the stage to a heroes' welcome, fully justified by opening track 'The Middle', built around a lament that strikes a familiar chord with anyone who works hard and plays harder, 'Now I know why I'm feeling so low/the nights go fast and the days go slow'.

Birmingham is blessed with a plethora of charismatic frontmen at the minute (Pearce Macca of The Clause and Connor Hill from The Novus are prime examples), but band leaders with the sheer, unadulterated swagger of George Johnson are as rare as hen's teeth, and by the time he's asserting, 'There's gold in me/one day you'll see', he's already preaching to the choir.

'Uptown', the lead single from their new *Dream Nights* EP, is a standard, uplifting Ivory Wave tune – it just happens to be their best one – but 'Cool Kids' and 'Weigh Me Down' aren't far behind in the anthemic, singalong stakes. Trust me, these boys know how to construct a chorus.

The melancholic beginning of 'Young Blood' signals a welcome breather for the mosh pit, but the respite is short-lived and we're soon back in absolute limbs territory as 'Separate Beat' gets an airing. The band wear their Britpop heart on their sleeve on this one, but George wittily pre-empts any lazy criticism – 'I know you/you know me/sounds like something from the mid-nineties'.

IVORY WAVE. (© PHIL DRURY, 2324 PHOTOGRAPHY)

They finish with the euphoric 'Club', and it's scenes on toast as they are roared off stage even more enthusiastically than they were roared on. They occasionally remind me of a certain Manchester band – someone rather cruelly referred to them as 'Ivory Mondays' to me recently – but so what? The Jam sounded a bit like the Who, Oasis sounded a bit like the Beatles. It didn't stop them from becoming two of the biggest and best bands of all time.

For the millennials and Gen Zs who make up the vast majority of the music-buying, streaming and gig-going public, these bands are a distant memory. I well remember the excitement of thinking the revolution might be televised after all, when the Mondays appeared on the same episode of *Top of the Pops* as the Stone Roses back in the eighties, but kids today will have only seen that if their parents watch old episodes on UK Gold, or if they googled Shaun Ryder when he was on *I'm A Celebrity*.

The truth is, if you're influenced by hedonism and house beats, or pills, thrills and Frankie Knuckles, you'll have a job NOT to sound like the Mondays – especially if you've got a similar talent for writing banging, anthemic choruses and you're an absolute lad like George Johnson. Ivory Wave encapsulate a feeling that's as fresh as a winter dawn for every generation lucky enough to experience it, and if you're the cynical type who's seen it all before, stop whining about your lost youth and try reliving it instead. Ivory Wave are here to help.

There's still time for me to catch the last, superb, half-hour of Call Me Unique and Madi Saskia at Mama Roux's, and after that, I'm tempted further up Lower Trinity Street to all-night soul club the Night Owl, helplessly led astray by the memorable Ivory Wave refrain that's still ringing in my ears … 'I'm Uptown … I'm not coming home tonight'.

POST-ELECTION (RHYTHM AND) BLUES

It hasn't even been a week since the building blocks of modern Birmingham – innovation and diversity – were defecated on from a great height by voters in the general election, and I've spent the early days of the new far-right government deleting people who voted for them from my socials. (They say it's a secret ballot, but it ain't just Mark Zuckerberg who knows you better than your family, just from your Facebook likes.) So, as The Jam said in the No. 1 hit that greeted the election of Thatcher back in the day, 'I'm Going Underground'; withdrawing from this wicked new world into a comfort bunker of multinational, multi-racial, multi-generational, cross-pollinated culture – or as I like to call it, Digbeth, where Brummies, be they born here or adopted, gather together to enjoy each other's food, dance to each other's music, bump each other's fists and hold each other's hands.

It's No Country For Old Tories and that suits me just fine. So, if anything can beat these post-election blues, it's a combination of B5 and a Birmingham Music Awards party …

THE BIRMINGHAM MUSIC AWARDS CHRISTMAS PARTY @ MAMA ROUX'S

When these events began, free to enter and showcasing ten new local acts every month, pessimists said it couldn't be done. But the organisers scoffed at the cynics because, plotted up where they are, right in amongst the local music scene, they knew the talent was there in abundance, and every month so far (this is the tenth event), they've been proved resoundingly right.

It's a music and networking opportunity par excellence; the place is awash with artists (whether they're performing or not), making connections with sponsors, A & Rs and labels, rubbing shoulders with promoters, venue managers and music colleges, swapping socials with bloggers, vloggers and journos. It's the Birmingham music version of the national grid, and it's hugely beneficial for any local act to be plugged in.

Meanwhile, actually ON the stage, magic happens. Life gets in the way of the six o'clock start time, hence I miss singer-songwriter Jessie Dipper and Dariusz Zaltash's alt-rock Emo project Cellar Door, but I'm sure I'll get round to them eventually. I arrive just in time to catch a powerful burst of North Parade's set, and then it's time for the two main reasons I'm here, instead of 100 yards away at the Mill watching B-Town behemoths Swim Deep and JAWS.

First, Kings Heath kids Cage Park smash out a five-song set with their customary panache, then 15-year-old Lea Hall phenomenon T.Roadz shells the stage with his machine gun grime bars and ridiculously dexterous flows. This teenage rampage tag team is a hard pair of acts to follow, but if anyone can, Ruth Noah can.

She's beefed up her sound since last I saw her by assembling The Ark, a five-piece band that could give the Black Eyed Peas lessons in diversity. There's a Vietnamese girl playing the funkiest guitar this side of the Nile (Rodgers), an incredible bass player who brings a whole new meaning to the term 'happy slapping', a percussionist with more energy than a gallon of Red Bull, and a drummer and saxophone player who look and sound like they've been kidnapped from *The Commitments*. They'd be worth seeing even if they were Ruth-less, but thank the Lord they're not.

Her slender frame gives no indication of what's to come, and she opens her mouth to unleash a voice direct from heaven, but with all the fire and brimstone of the other place. Mum and Dad glimpsed the future when they gave her a biblical name, because this is a biblical performance, and it makes you wonder which Birmingham you're in – UK or Alabama.

I only know one song, a cover of Ike and Tina Turner's 'Funkier than a Mosquito's Tweeter' (and it is), but I'll be getting to know Ruth's original numbers ASAP. Jools Holland would love her, and she'd go down a storm at mod/soul weekenders in scooter rally season. Other highlights include the wavy rhythms and slick rhymes of Mr Macee (pronounced 'Macky'), his storming collaboration with the king of Kingstanding, Mayday, and Beasey, a more intense version of Sleaford Mods' Jason Williamson, if that's even possible.

Courthouse and their many fans who stay right to the death ensure the night ends on a high. Their set peaks with a Nina Simone cover that would have the high priestess of soul herself dancing in her grave, and thanks mainly to Ruth Noah, and despite the fact that it's a new dawn and a new day and a new, terrible government, I'm feeling good.

SANTA CLAUSE

This particular Saturday night was a big one in Birmingham. UB40 were playing the Arena, The Wonder Stuff, the big room at the Academy, and there was a great Small Faces tribute act on at my favourite club, the Night Owl. The music of all three is prominent on the soundtrack to my life, and I have personal connections with some of the personnel.

Spoilt for choice? Nah. There's nothing wrong with a bit of nostalgia now and again but I'd rather look forward, and The Clause's future is so bright I gotta wear shades, even if they do look silly in this terrible rain.

THE CLAUSE @ O2 ACADEMY

I jump through the necessary hoops to collect my tickets from the box office – photo ID, the card I paid with, confirmation email – when did it all get so complicated? – and I'm probably at the door long enough to miss a couple of acts. I finally make it through in time to see The Assist, the main support, whose passionately delivered 'council pop' is well received by the 650-capacity crowd.

The Black Country boys have not long returned from playing several shows in Russia alongside The Twang, and their danceable yet powerful singles 'Just a Dream Away' and 'I Don't Care' carry a hard-hitting hint of their recent touring partners' sound. When the occasional keyboards kick in there's an Editors vibe going on, and the band exude a passionate and fiercely working-class West Midlands persona.

They exit the stage to cheers, having doubtless won over a few new fans, me included. Excitement is building nicely for the headliners, whipped up during the interval by a host of timeless classics like 'Morning Glory' and 'A Town Called Malice'; you don't tease a crowd with a playlist like that unless you're confident you can match it with your own songs, and The Clause most certainly can. They cut their teeth as a live band covering tunes like this – now their originals are on a par with them.

Lights go out in *el teatro* and the sound of Samuel L. Jackson's pre-killing-spree speech from *Pulp Fiction* fills the room, while the shadowy figures of the band take the stage under flickering strobe lights. First, Liam unleashes the relentless riff of 'Tokyo', then Niall's drums and Jonny's bass kick and throb respectively into action, and it all pops off in the mosh pit. These boys certainly know how to make an entrance. 'Golden Age' is next, Pearce's cutting lyrics mixing social commentary and a sly dig at that nostalgia I was on about: 'Darlin' I ain't from the golden age/I'm getting drunk scraping by on the minimum wage'.

'Dig this Beat' is a party piece, but still contains a first verse and a chorus most bands would kill for, and the throwaway feel continues as 'Hate the Player' merges into Abba's 'Gimme! Gimme! Gimme!' There sings a man at ease with his sexuality. I've gone off The Who a bit since hearing about Townshend's 'research' and Daltrey coming out as a Brexiter (the other two are dead, like Roger's brain), but regardless, it was nice to hear a nod to them in the form of the riff from 'So Sad About Us', which powers the brilliant 'Comedown Conversations'. Lots of the very best bands announce themselves with a truly great debut single – I'm thinking The Clash, The Jam, Oasis, Arctic Monkeys – and The Clause certainly ticked this box in 2016 with 'Shut me Out', which boasts the kind of beautifully melancholic lyrics that are beyond most songwriters throughout their careers, never mind a 16/17-year-old as Pearce was when he wrote it. 'It's strange to see you again/ I feel there's something missing/I don't wanna hear you say/Anything you don't mean.' Marvellous.

The pace slows on 'Vive la Revolucion', giving Liam the time to finesse his guitar-god poses. He really is a gig photographer's dream. Pearce dedicates 'Where are you Now?' to anybody who's lost someone recently, which is particularly poignant for one of our party, Gay Morse, who's wonderful son Ben was the tragic victim of a hit-and-run incident last year. Suddenly, the room seems roomier as virtually half the people in it are on somebody's shoulders.

The band only have to play the first few chords before we sing the first verse for them, Pearce occasionally helping us out on harmonies, before two backing singers arrive on stage for a seasonal 'Happy Christmas (War Is Over)'. Jesus, they're covering Lennon now and it doesn't even stand out.

Lyrical masterpiece 'Sixteen' is next before the song that tempted Universal to sign the band a couple of months ago, 'In my Element' gives us the mosh-pit moment of the night as Santa Claus goes crowd surfing. He'd have a difficult time getting the right presents for The Clause – what do you give to the band that has everything?

Work in the morning rules out the Snobs after-party, and as I head home in the back of an A2B, I'm elated about the night, but worried about the review, because I'm quite simply lost for words. I can barely think of enough for a homeward bound tweet: 'Gig of the millennium. Simple.'

AGENTS DOUBLE-O SOUL

Soul music was my first love, but once I'd been unfaithful to her with The Jam and The Clash, there was no stopping me. I've since had flirtations with indie and grime, agit-pop and hip-hop, acid-jazz and Nick Drake, but I'll never tire of my first love – particularly when she comes to town, just a ten-minute train ride away, and I don't have to get up for work in the morning …

NAMYWA, RUTH NOAH AND THE ARK @ THE SUNFLOWER LOUNGE

It's rare and refreshing to see this under-represented genre getting some airtime, so kudos to Discover Birmingham, a month-long celebratory showcase of local talent put together by Birmingham Promoters, BBC *Introducing* and Counteract, all taking place at the legendary Sunflower Lounge. The curators had evidently got hold of my algorithms and, on the same bill, put two of the vanishingly small number of artists who could tempt me – nay, force me – through sheer magnetism, to abandon Dry January on a freezing cold night when I'm at that special post-Christmas level of skint.

First up is Ruth Noah, a pocket dynamo with a voice that could fill (and rattle the windows of) a room much bigger than the sold-out 200-capacity one she's playing tonight. She's not alone, of course, having recently assembled a fantastic band, The Ark, co-conspirators in bringing her musical vision to reality.

They open with a dramatic intro and an appropriate tribute to rhythm and blues royalty Ike and Tina Turner, with a storming version of 'Funkier than a Mosquito's Tweeter'. Ruth's own sound is a direct descendent of Ike and his Kings of Rhythm, and on this form, she's next in line to the throne. There's a hint of Amy Winehouse about her phrasing, which is fair enough as Amy culturally appropriated her style from black music in the first place, but for the rest of the set, Ruth's voice is as deep and dirty as Louisiana mud, with the grit and growl of a female Tom Waits, occasionally lashing out in the style of classic soul shouters like Big Maybelle.

Songs like 'Ruby', 'Woman' and 'Fire' go right back to the birth of soul, when blues got together with gospel and conceived a genre that was, in my opinion, the greatest cultural achievement of the twentieth century – the fact that Ruth is so damn good at it says it all. She finishes with a song called '1960' which, rather appropriately, fits the musical timeline I'm on about, although this music isn't old-fashioned – it's timeless.

As we cheer her and the band off, I explain to my young black mate that there is a lucrative crossover audience for brilliantly realised pure soul like this among mods and scooter boys, and he gets it straight away: 'Yeah, look at those white people at the front, they're loving it!'

RUTH NOAH. (© TAYLOR WRIGHT @TAYSHOTYOU)

Top of the bill is Namywa, with a sound that is uncompromisingly twenty-first century, but no less soulful for that. Ian Silk on guitar gets things under way with the relentless groove of 'Wound Up', while Namywa adds the stream-of-consciousness bars that are her lyrical trademark. The driving beat of 'Let me Treat you Right' gives way to the joyful swing of 'Only the Sweetest' – yet more unconventional and enchanting words that are testament to Namywa's pen game.

'Summer's Night in June' imaginatively and poetically sets a host of common usage abbreviations to the thrilling music, and she gets all assertive on the strident 'Get to Know me Again'. 'A Woman Like me' is a new one to my ears, and I'm pleased to hear she's lost none of her appetite for trusting her audience with her personality and truth.

Next up is a gorgeous new ballad, 'Home', during which I get a bit carried away and put my lighter up. (I may have been the first, but I very much doubt I'll be the last.) Achingly beautiful and emotionally resonant, it makes me come over all unnecessary, the fragility in her voice as she pleads, 'I don't think my heart's that strong' … well, I can't speak for the house, but there isn't a dry eye in my head.

Another new one, 'A Little Freedom', makes its live debut and provides more evidence that the song-writing camp she went on recently is paying handsome dividends, and her blistering cover of Eminem's 'Lose Yourself' – how's that for ambition? – is fast becoming a live favourite. This is followed by her soaring, singalong anthem 'Jungle' – she's just showing off now.

The show closes with magnificently sweaty funk workout 'Matter of Fact' and, like Namywa, I'm done.

When the cast of hundreds on the two dozen Discover Birmingham shows was announced last month and I had to pick only one night, it was a tortuously difficult decision. It helped that they put two of the best on the same bill, and I think I called it. Ladies … your Birmingham Music Awards nominations are in.

BIG IN SEOUL

I'm sitting on the last bus out of town, looking at a blank page on my phone notes, wondering if I know enough superlatives to describe what I've just witnessed. With the help of an online thesaurus, I can but try … so wish me luck.

KARKOSA AND NORTH PARADE @ MAMA ROUX'S

Valentine's Day is a big deal in our house, coinciding as it does with Wifey's birthday the next day, so we spent a long weekend celebrating in Dublin. We did the tours, the romantic dinners, watched the Villa on telly and drank gallons of Guinness in a live music bar, at which the singer/guitarist on the small stage requested requests. Feeling a bit homesick, I asked for some Birmingham music, hoping for Dexy's Midnight Runners (too difficult apparently) and settling for Ocean Colour Scene. Everybody sang along and indulged in some Peaky Blinders-based 'bantz', and it was all good fun in a beautiful city – full of friendly people, but a bit monocultural compared to home. Hence, there was an extra spring in my step when I got back and walked through my own Irish Quarter towards some great Brummie indie that's big in Korea.

Karkosa have been working hard over the last couple of years to make their presence felt on the vibrant local music scene, but despite having a much-documented and passionate following in South Korea, South Yardley and its environs were proving a tougher nut to crack. In an attempt to remedy this, they followed the shining example of local heroes The Nu and The Novus by promoting their own DIY show at Mama Roux's on Wednesday night.

I arrived at the newly refurbished venue just in time to see North Parade's support slot, opening with hometown homage 'Birmingham' (yeah, that's the name of the song), the frontman channelling Sandie Shaw as he kicked off his shoes to perform. This Bob Dylan fan loved his harmonica playing on 'Feminism', and 'Keep Things Casual' is a real ear-worm.

They rounded off a fine set with their latest single, the critically acclaimed 'An Accommodation', inspired by the Simon Armitage poem of the same name and driven along by some fantastic drumming. There's even a nifty reference to the Bull Ring in the lyrics, towards which the frontman accurately points during the relevant line.

A quick vape, a refreshed pint and it was time for the headliners' line-up of band leader Michael Warnock, his brother Jack (drums), Tom Rushton (guitar), Isabelle Florence (bass), Will Clews (keyboards) and Pete Donnelly (just about everything) to be greeted enthusiastically by a packed house.

The gig is to mark the release of new single 'The Rival', and the song gets the show off to a lively start. It's a typical example of the melodic pop-rock at which the band excel – epic in scale, going off on proggy tangents involving brass and synthesisers, with soaring choruses and dramatic swoops of tempo and volume. This descriptive cap fits most of their repertoire – 'Mango Tree', 'Where the River Flows' and 'Aurora' are highlights, along with new B-side, 'Runaway', the lyrics of which reference a yearning to be in Florida because 'there's no theme parks here at home'. Come on Michael, you're from Sutton mate – never been to Thomas Land?

It all comes together most effectively on 'Red Hoodie' and 'Sheffield', two adrenaline-fuelled anthems of adolescent melodrama, soaked in catchy melodies and teenage angst. The band and crowd are by now having an equally great time, with inflatable trees bouncing round the mosh pit, Tom smiling more than the Joker as he coaxes magic from his Flying-V guitar, and Pete switching effortlessly between trumpet, keyboards and tambourine while careering across the stage like a talented version of Bez from the Happy Mondays.

The songs are meaty, beaty, big and bouncy, but there's considerable versatility on offer – 'The Devil's Greatest Trick' is so heavy in places it's a timely reminder that it's the fiftieth anniversary of Black Sabbath's debut album, and a new song, 'Seoul', is a slow burner that showcases perfectly the amazing voice of new (ish) member, Isabelle. Instantly recognisable as a truly great piece of music, it has people nearby asking me if it's an original number or a cover of some multi-platinum-selling household name.

The lighters go up, the phone torches are on display, and as the crowd chants, 'One more song', at the end of the set, the band have little choice but to play it again. It's a show that catapults Karkosa onto the top table of Birmingham indie, but this song, if they can get enough ears on it, could take them a whole lot further. As he left the stage, Michael informs us that we were the best crowd ever – which, from a guy who's played to 400 hysterical Koreans, comes as quite a compliment to 200 reserved Brummies. I'm not sure how true it is, but I'll take it.

GO WEST, YOUNG MEN

A dream line-up for me, the last before lockdown...

THE NOVUS, CAGE PARK, THE NEW CONSISTENT @ MOTHER'S RUIN, BRISTOL

When the date and line-up was announced, even though it was on a Sunday night in Bristol, an entry was made in the diary, all in capitals and underlined with passionate determination. The night before a 6 a.m. start at work? I booked it off. No cash two days before payday? I'll take the credit card. Leaving Wifey at home on the only day we're at home together all week? Get in the good books by taking her to Dublin the week before.

The best-laid plans of mice and men were made weeks ago ... and it was all worth it. I arrive at the venue in plenty of time and can relax with a pint or two as the bands cart their gear downstairs to the basement venue and panic over the late arrival of the soundman. All's well that ends well, though, and apparently, he's a quick worker, good at his job and friendly to boot. In fact, he's sound, man, and everything is set up in time for The New Consistent to take the stage just a few minutes behind schedule.

While Brad Sumner skilfully supplies samples, beats and myriad sound effects courtesy of a laptop connected to what looks like a mini-mixing desk, wordsmith Ben Ramsay raps a series of kitchen sink dramas with understated lyrical elegance. On songs like 'Rude Boys', 'Three Years' and 'Greta Oto', he explores the dysfunctional relationships of families, lovers and friends, mining magic from the mundane, while offering us an escape route via the melodic and infectious choruses of 'Turn Off All the Screens' and the song from which he takes his name, 'The New Consistent'. It's intelligent and challenging stuff, full of character and personality, and I love it.

Ever since I first heard Cage Park a couple of years ago, I've been clucking like a crack head for each new song they write, so I'm delighted as they take the tiny stage and open with fresh banger 'Kitchen Floor', which on first listen comfortably clears the incredibly high bar set by their previous releases. Their versatile sound can be as poppy as bubble wrap or as grungy as Nirvana – sometimes, like on 'Castle of Cards', in the same song. Leo's brilliant guitar playing is angular and discordant and reminiscent of a young Wilko Johnson, while Edie's bass and Reuben's drums power along like the Arctic Monkeys rhythm section on a runaway train.

Frontman Arthur is the lightning rod – energised by the electricity surrounding him into dancing frantically while delivering eloquent and intricate lyrics with dexterity and tenderness and a cry in his voice. He takes over on bass as Edie voices a feisty version of Taylor Swift's 'We Are Never Ever Getting Back Together', and the pair dovetail perfectly when duetting on 'Tunnel Vision', 'Parma Violets' and 'Lightning', with its *Happy Days* handclaps and a chorus as catchy as COVID-19.

THE NEW CONSISTENT. (© PAUL MOREAU)

Talking of viruses, The Novus take the stage with lead singer Connor Hill looking and singing as though he's been catching microbes of the Rage virus from watching *28 Days Later* too often. With the venue resembling an oversized coffin, there's a distinctly dystopian feel to the gig and the headliners provide the perfect soundtrack. Described recently by Gigslutz as 'the art raged grandchildren of Black Sabbath' (wish I'd thought of that), the comparison is hinted at by opening number 'I Serve Not', compounded by 'Post-Modern Fairytale', and confirmed by 'New Age'. Seeing them live is an unforgettable experience. Connor oozes charisma and spits pure bile; Tom Rhodes and Tyla Challenger (on lead and bass guitars respectively) frame and complement him perfectly, and drummer Euan Woodman drives the whole show from the rear as he bangs the bass drum with a foot like a traction engine.

Latest single 'Frosty' is a real highlight. After a screech of feedback that's enough to clear any unwanted pets from the room, Tom's guitar (it sounds like he's playing three) crunches into the tune proper and we're away. Tyla's reimagining of the epic bassline from Paul Weller's 'Porcelain Gods' is a depth charge that could shatter porcelain, and Connor spits and snarls disdain for the other party in a shattered relationship.

Fevered and fiery are the order of the night, and a stunning cover of Billy Eilish's 'The Crown' is the only non-original song in a set that proves just how prolific The Novus are with their own ideas, with 'Overdrive' and 'Pigs' bringing the show, not so much to a close, more a crescendo.

Someone commented to me recently that they're 'too political' – nonsense. They certainly wear their radical hearts on their (left) sleeves, but I think it's about time rock found its conscience again and stopped leaving it up to grime and rap. It was a great gig, with some fantastic repping for the Birmingham music scene, and if you had to pick three emerging acts to showcase the best of new Brum-based music in a strange town, you'd be hard-pressed to improve on this trio.

When lockdown took hold, and the live scene ground to a halt, I was a bit stuck for things to write about. Luckily for me, people were still making records and wanting to talk about them …

23 June 2016 – a fateful date on which a decision was made that will impact lives for years to come. Two of Birmingham's most promising musicians were in Harborne watching another one – Ed Geater – and as they reclined in the beer garden of the Plough, they decided to ring the young singer they had recently jammed with and offer her the front-woman role in their band.

Genie Mendez had replied to an advert placed by Alex Lowe and Charlie Kellie and made quite an impression on them, and when Alex offered her the gig, she readily accepted, and the soulful electro-pop trio, Lycio was formed. Oh, and there was some big vote as well. I spoke to Alex to find out more …

First things first … what did the advert say?

I actually found an original advert still up on a noticeboard a few weeks ago but it's in Robannas studio in town, so I'll have to have a look next time. It was also online … I believe the Facebook group West Midlands Bands and Musicians was where Genie replied to. I remember we said we needed someone who could write great lyrics and melodies – we referenced Alt-J and Genie loves them. She says that's what made her reply. The funny thing is that only last year she confessed that she wasn't convinced after that first jam … like she wasn't feeling it, and when we rang her and said, 'We'd love you to join', she was kind of like, 'Oh …', like she wasn't convinced. But luckily, she gave it a go and the rest is history.

Were there any other contenders?

Yes, but we jammed with Genie first and we were so convinced we said yes to her before we saw the other person. We decided that we'd jam with them anyway as we'd already agreed and wanted to honour that, but she said she wasn't feeling the genre and vibe so there was no bad feeling.

So does Genie write all the lyrics then?

Yeah, she writes all the lyrics and melodies while Charlie and myself write the music.

What are your musical backgrounds?

Charlie did music tech/popular music/composition at Huddersfield Uni, Genie went to the BOA performing arts school in Eastside, and I went to BIMM in Brighton and did a professional diploma in drums and then professional musicianship. It's like a reverse of how we originally grew up, because Charlie was originally a drummer – a very good one – and I was a classical person. Violin was my first instrument and I played guitar, so we've almost swapped roles compared to our teenage selves.

And Genie famously worked at the Sunflower Lounge for a while …

Yeah, she worked at the Sunny but that was a little after we started. She was in the in-between phase of college and going to uni when she got in contact with us about our advert. She was gonna go to Derby uni to do sound tech I think, but she was deferring the place by a year or so and by the time that came round she decided she didn't want to go – which was lucky for me and Charlie! We were already two or three years graduated from our music degrees, so we were in different phases of our lives when we started the group.

It's been a while since 'Saharan King' blew me away and there haven't been loads of songs since then. Are you perfectionists?

Haha, we are, yeah! After 'Saharan' we did 'Evil People' and then we did three songs where we engineered, mixed and produced ourselves – 'Cash', 'Young Ties' and 'Up Down'. The process slowed us down a bit but we learned a lot, so it was worthwhile.

Your current single 'Nightfall' looks and sounds like a really topical comment on the COVID crisis.

Yeah, 'Nightfall' definitely looks like that – as we always try to put a visual together for every track, and because we were limited due to the situation, Charlie borrowed his brother's GoPro and cycled around the deserted streets filming. We've had this kind of double single release of 'Nightfall' / 'Somebody' planned since around September last year but I worry that people will think we released the tracks in this way because of the lockdown, when in fact we've had it planned for a long time. We wrote both songs in February of last year, in the same week, so they feel like cousins!

'Somebody' is a more upbeat one. Musically, it's more groovy, but Genie wrote it about unrequited love; so it's lyrically fairly open. Usually her stuff is a little more ambiguous and often related to mental health issues.

Is there a visual for that one, too?

Yeah, I've surprised Charlie and Genie with this one actually and put together a memory video. We were collecting all of our Lycio memories, initially to use on social media during this lockdown for some fun content, and it occurred to me to make a montage. Partly to reminisce about past fun times and to look forward to when we can tour again; and also, as the song is about unrequited love, it's a nice visual to represent friendship and that kind of love.

I've seen the version you performed for Sofar Sounds …

Ah yeah, the acoustic version. I love watching Sofar Sounds shows – it's such an iconic platform and I think you can often see bands looking a little more sweaty than usual, and concentrating more than they usually do! I kind of see it as a Jools Holland for up and coming bands – you don't wanna mess it up! We have a healthy number of dislikes on that video – I kind of like that because it's good to provoke a strong reaction!

You must have had big live plans around your double single release before this damn lockdown?

We were going to be playing Mello Festival and the Bear Tavern for Bear Grooves later this year, and we also had a gig with a band called Beautiful Little Fools at the Victoria planned, but they disbanded because of the whole situation at the moment apparently. I was gutted for them because they had loads of potential.

Yes, that's a real shame, they were certainly off to a promising start. Named after a great Jorja Smith song, too.

Yeah, it was a great name! I'm hoping they reconsider and start up again sometime soon. We've got an as-of-yet unannounced headline show though for later in the year and another two tracks to be released so we're realigning for later this year!

It's good to hear that you're not getting TOO derailed by it all.

Yeah, we're pretty productive so we're good at finding things to do. We've worked around this period as best we can. We started recording stems just before the lockdown, for releases in 2021 so we've been pretty busy working remotely on those.

One more thing – where did the name come from?

Haha! Unfortunately the name is a secret, sorry! It's origin has been our best-kept secret!

No exclusive then?

It's such a ridiculous way that we thought of it … we're not sure we'll ever be able to bring ourselves to tell anyone!

Don't worry readers, I'll get them drunk after lockdown finishes and have them singing like canaries!

SIREN VOICE

A few weeks ago, in what now seems like another world, local indie heroes La Dharma were looking forward to playing a series of dates in support of their new single, 'Devils'. Then you-know-what came along and derailed their plans, as well of those of the whole live music scene and … well, everything else really. Cold comfort perhaps, but at least the internet is still up and running, meaning that I can conduct remote interviews I had planned with up-and-coming rock stars – very useful for getting the La Dharma lowdown from lead singer Chris Leedham.

This is a terrible situation for everyone, not least musicians. How has it affected La Dharma in particular?

Well I think it's just put things on hold for everybody hasn't it? So many people are being affected by it all and obviously health comes first, so we all need to concentrate on that and help each other where we can. I'm sure I'll be annoying the guys with awful alcohol-induced song ideas I've come up with during a night of isolated drinking before long though, I've been guilty of that before. They very rarely tend to make it to the studio.

The songs or the guys?

No! The songs! The guys usually make it most of the time.

Glad to hear! Where did the name come from?

Jonah, our guitarist, read a book by Jack Kerouac called the Dharma Bums, then he looked up the meaning of Dharma and there was no official meaning for it in any western language, which we quite liked. We just added the 'La' to make it sound a bit French.

'Sirens' made quite a big impression on me when it was released. Where does that one sit in the La Dharma timeline?

It was the first single with the current line-up and was always designed to kind of set the scene for the first EP, if you like.

I've had a listen to the new one. It rattles along at a good pace, with powerful, distinctive vocals and the trademark La Dharma storming chorus. As Tim Senna might say, it slaps harder than a Saturday night fight on Broad Street.

Thanks so much. A chorus is always going to be the make or break on whether somebody listens to the next verse I guess, so that's good to hear.

Most bands take a while to find their voice. It's amazing how quickly you've established your sound.

Our sound was just kind of something that happened when blending all of our musical interests. I think we've found the type of music we want to make so it's sure to be a continued theme with the music we put out this year. Feels like there is a lot of space for variety which we tried to get across in the first EP.

Yeah, I loved the EP, but don't rest on your laurels, tell me about the new one!

The new song's called 'Devils' and it's one we've had for a while to be honest. We've recently re-written it to try and give the melodies as much of an impact as the opening guitar riff and just decided it was ready to be released now. So yeah, people that have been kind enough to come and see us play live over the last year or so will hopefully recognise it. As far as the meaning behind the song, it's basically about that little devil you get on your shoulder that causes you to romanticise things that you maybe shouldn't.

The lyrics are important to you, aren't they?

Yeah definitely, lyrics are massively important to us. I always struggle to just settle on lyrics and sometimes have had to re-record them after last-minute changes. I like the idea of linking songs together as well, so there's a lot of references to previous songs and stuff so every song has a reason and it's all a bit of an ongoing story.

Sounds like there might be a concept album one day, maybe?

Yeah, that's certainly the plan!

Who do you look up to as lyricists and songwriters?

I'm personally a big 1975 fan and especially the lyricism of Matt Healy, I find their song writing very honest. Van McCann and more recently Sam Fender always engage me with their lyrics as well. Then going back a bit, Ian Curtis, especially after watching 'Control'.

I always see you at gigs in town — you seem to make an effort to support other local bands. Is there anyone in particular you rate?

Yeah of course, there's so many I rate, which is why I'm at so many gigs! If I was going to pick one out, I'd have to say The Nu, they've had a great year and the headline show they did at Mama Roux's was my favourite show of last year.

Finally, then, and back on topic, how does the La Dharma magic come together?

Lyrics, vocal and synth melodies are usually me, but the whole song-writing process is a collective thing with everybody's input. Sometimes we'll have a particular riff that Jonah [guitar] has written and build a song around that, or sometimes I'll take a song in and the lads will bring it to life. James and Boothy always write their own parts as well, on drums and bass. Then it's a case of making sure the song has its part in the La Dharma story. We've got a fair few written that just don't fit at the minute either contextually or musically. I can be quite guilty of trying to push forward with songs that I relate to at that particular time.

So it's a bit like Peace then? As Harri Koisser puts it — 'I plant the seeds and the rest of the boys fertilise it.'

Haha! I'd prefer to say, 'I plant the bulb and the boys bring the rain and the sun.'

Perhaps that explains why La Dharma have grown on me (sorry).

LIVING IT UP
IN LOCKDOWN

In 2017, Darius Zaltash briefly gave up on his dream of a career in music by dropping out of his course at the British and Irish Modern Music Institute in Brighton and moving back home to Reading to work a 9–5 job. By the time BIMM opened their new campus in Birmingham, he was ready to give it another go, and is now the driving force behind one of the city's most dynamic and promising bands, The Nu. I caught up with Darius ahead of the release of their new single, 'One Life', to hear about his story so far …

The Nu are a sort of Brum-indie supergroup, aren't they?

Yeah, basically! I do all the writing and recording of the songs myself and then I have a session band which consists of Tom from Karkosa, Ollie who plays for Stella and various other bands, and Conor from The Pines. We like to work as a group on the live show, though, just to spice things up a bit.

Will there be a tug-of-love over those guys when all your nationwide tours clash?

Hahaha, possibly! I just run the dates by them way in advance and if they're free then they confirm. If not, I sometimes get back-up members in.

I spoke to Lycio recently, who's singer Genie, like you, worked at the Sunflower Lounge. Are there any more budding superstars behind the bar?

Yes definitely. I worked with Fergus Channell and he's got one of the best voices in Brum in my opinion, a seriously talented guy. I would definitely recommend listening to him. Lycio are sick by the way!

What are you most looking forward to doing again, post-apocalypse?

Ooooh, good question. I guess it's gotta be playing shows again, or even just rehearsing. I really miss going to local shows as well, you can't beat live music and a Red Stripe!

What about the barbers?

I'm growing my hair out at the moment so luckily managed to spend a lot of the 'in-between phase' in lockdown. I think it may be a while before I get another trim!

On to the music then … what inspires your lyrics?

I think the main thing I like to do with my lyrics is to put the listener in the shoes of whatever the song is about, so if it's a relationship, either personal or not, I try to put the listener in the head of the person whose thoughts and emotions are being expressed. If it's mental health or politics, I tend to not beat around the bush, to actually say what I believe should be said, but still be artistic.

THE NU. (© LEE CRAWFORD, DISTORTED IMAGE PHOTOGRAPHY)

I like lyrics that take you on a journey from start to finish, even if only when you are listening carefully or looking up the lyrics online. I think people get sucked into the idea that in order to tell a story every part of it must have its own moment in the light, but sometimes having two different verses and the same chorus can be more powerful than switching the words around in order to make the picture more obvious. The song can still say what you want it to say, but also say things you didn't expect by leaving it up to the listener to interpret.

What were your musical influences growing up?

There were a lot of different types of music playing around the house. We had a record player in the living room and the record my sister played me that I used to have on repeat was Led Zeppelin IV, and I think that was where my love of guitar music originated. My other sister would play more modern, heavier stuff from time to time, but mainly rave and electronic stuff. She had this massive stereo system and I remember the bass that came from it just blowing my mind. All this meant that the first band that I fully fell in love with and that resonated with me was Linkin Park. The electronic/guitar crossover just felt so powerful and paved the way for a lot of the music I would listen to and is still the band I'd say influenced me most.

Who do you look up to now?

I think lyrically Chester Bennington, Rou Reynolds, Matt Healy and Tom Delonge. I think they're all musical genii sound-wise as well. I have to say Michael Hutchence and Perry Farrell for just how incredible they were/are as frontmen.

Why did you drop out of BIMM Brighton?

I deferred the year for medical reasons then decided to drop out soon after. It was to do with my mental health – it deteriorated over the course of that year for various reasons, and the rock and roll lifestyle didn't help.

So how did you end up in Brum?

I was at home working in Reading and decided I wanted to go to uni again after watching a programme called Fresh Meat, which made me proper miss the whole uni atmosphere. I saw an advert for BIMM Birmingham which had just opened, and it just seemed like a good move to make, taking what I learned in Brighton and applying it to a smaller college but a bigger city.

Did you have any preconceptions before you arrived?

To be honest before I moved to Birmingham, I didn't know a lot about it, except it was the second biggest in the UK and that JAWS, Peace and Sabbath were from here! I kind of wanted to keep it a mystery until I arrived, I thought it would make me want to go and explore. When I got here, the first thing I did was go to a gig at the Sunflower Lounge cos BIMM put out a 'what's on' guide and I'd heard of the Sunny after a friend's band played there. The two bands who played that night were La Dharma and MARC, incredible acts. I absolutely adored them and some of the members have become some of my closest friends in the city.

A good first impression, then. What do you think now you know it better?

After going to more shows and meeting more people the impression I've formed of Birmingham is that it's an anomaly in the UK. The sense of community here is like no other place I've experienced, and the outstandingly wide range of musical talent is incredible. It baffles me how much is going on here which I didn't know about! I feel like some people overlook Birmingham and think that the hubs of music in the UK are Manchester and London, but I have a strong and growing feeling that will be over very soon.

See? I told you – it's not just me.

And then, for me at least, live music was back for one night only …

THE TWANG, THE CLAUSE @ THE BRITISH OAK, STIRCHLEY

With the deadline for this worthy tome just weeks away, I was desperate to review a Twang show. It would be ludicrous to publish a book about the Birmingham music scene over recent years with no mention of the city's best band during that time. And so it was that I found myself walking home from work the day this gig was announced, head in phone, trying to book tickets.

At that (very inopportune) moment, a friend pulled up offering a lift. Not wishing to appear rude I put my phone away, only to find, ten short minutes later, that the gig had sold out while I was in transit. Not to worry, I know the band's long-time producer – the man, the myth, the legend – Gavin Monaghan. He did his best to sort me out, but in the end could only inform me that there was no guest list and The Twang's manager had given the last available table to the venue's bar staff.

Next desperate act – phone the pub. I asked if any of the staff didn't like the band and if so, could I take their pew at the staff table? I even offered to collect glasses or be a roadie for the day, but the answer was still no: table service only, and The Twang apparently have enough roadies already – including some who actually know what they're doing. How could I compete with that?

It had never previously crossed my mind that there were advantages to starting work at five in the morning, but you live and learn, and on the Friday before the gig I turned my phone on at 4.30 a.m. to see two tickets for sale on the internet. I was in like Flynn this time, with no distractions. I spent the rest of the day skipping around work with the band's brilliant back catalogue in my headphones, joyous in the knowledge that I was soon to break my Twang cherry at last.

Wifey and I made sure we arrived in plenty of time to see the Next Big Thing out of Brum, The Clause, and joined the boisterous queue, populated in part by a group of ticketless lads who seemed to have been enjoying the beer, wine and sunshine a little too much. They were bragging confidently that they'd get in, despite being advised to the contrary by some of the more sober folks waiting in line. Shouting rather rudely at the guys and girls checking tickets on the gate, they enquired about their chance of gaining admission, and after being told it was about the same as a snowball's in hell, stomped off full of bravado, shouting 'The Twang are crap anyway'.

For a moment, it seemed that a girl in the queue might come to their rescue when she said she had a spare ticket. The 'Twang are crap' mob almost fell over each other in the stampede. 'Sell it to me', 'No, me, I'll pay double face value'. She just laughed, gave them the finger and said sarcastically, 'But The Twang are crap though'.

The latest beneficiaries of the band's generous backing of local acts (they've previously given much-coveted support slots to Peace, JAWS and Sugarthief) are The Clause, who seized the opportunity with both hands. Opening with a new song, 'Time of our Lives', that promises much about their lockdown creativity, they grabbed the attention of the crowd with a cover of James' 'Laid'. Other highlights included Clause classics 'Comedown Conversations', '16', 'Where are you Now?' and 'In my Element' – and they really are classics. Great band, but some advice to anyone seeing them for the first time – go and see them when the rhythm section are present – they're a different beast.

When I fell in love with The Twang, I fell backwards. I had a copy of their first album, *Love it When I Feel Like This*, over a decade ago, but the bloke who lent it me was a bit of a div, so I didn't bother listening before I gave it back. As a consequence, I had remained ignorant of that brilliant debut and the rest of their mighty canon until quite recently, when I met singer Phil Etheridge at a Swim Deep gig. He struck me as refreshingly normal and a very humble and affable bloke.

I enthused about their song 'Everytime' and he told me a bit about the then-unreleased album that spawned it, *If Confronted Just Go Mad*. I bought it a few months later and felt like I did when I caught a random episode of *The Sopranos* – utterly compelled to go back to the beginning to find out how we got here.

There followed a real voyage of discovery – vibrant verses, singalong choruses, sophisticated and poetic lyrics; often humorous, but also brutally honest. The songs were stories in which you often recognised yourself, and not always in a complimentary way. Adult relationships were explored in vivid detail, minute mosaic tiles pieced painstakingly together until a big theme was revealed. Joy, desire, regret, despair – you name it, it was in there – and throughout the years the music had stayed as fresh as any debut album.

THE TWANG. (© LUKE JONES)

But my late arrival to the party meant I had never seen one of their legendary live gigs, and now, at long last, the wait was over. They took the stage to muted cheers and applause, possibly down to the understated entrance, or the fact that everyone was sitting down at a socially distanced table. Or maybe it's been so long since most of us went to a gig we've forgotten how to act?

But the crowd were soon enlivened by the first song, 'Wide Awake', even though the opening line, 'I feel the cold setting in' struck a chord in the autumn sunshine. They followed this up with a breezy 'Barney Rubble' from *Jewellery Quarter*, which for me is the best album ever to be named after a Birmingham suburb, just shading it from *Handsworth Revolution* by Steel Pulse and Ocean Colour Scene's *Moseley Shoals*.

The funky psychedelia of 'Dream' from the latest album was next, and as the sun disappeared, we could all relate to the song's setting 'in Handsworth Park in the middle of winter'. Enough labouring the point already – it was cold, okay?

The wistful vibe of 'Beer, Wine and Sunshine' is perfect for this format, but in truth, all the songs are so well crafted that they more than pass the stern test of an acoustic performance. Phil's voice positively flourishes in this setting, the immense talent of Stu and Ash on guitars is obvious and Jon's harmonising works a treat.

The audience begins to warm themselves up by singing along to 'Amsterdam' and the brilliant and affecting plea for Brummie unity (that's my interpretation anyway), 'We're a Crowd'. This is followed by 'It Feels Like', my favourite tune from *If Confronted*, with its almost Buddhist mantra, 'Til we find peace of mind, we will float like debris in the tide'.

A couple of months ago I posted a link to the next song, 'Mainline', with the caption, 'As if The Twang wrote a song about Coronavirus in 2013'. It was gratifying, therefore, to hear it introduced as 'our COVID song', the band obviously sharing my view of its relevance to the current crisis … 'bringing families to tears in the twilight years/ruining the nurtured seed'. Seriously, check out the whole song – it's uncanny.

The band's wonderful renditions of 'Life on a What If' and 'Got me Sussed' remind me of Sam Lambeth's perceptive description – 'they were heirs to the Smiths' suburban melancholia more than Oasis' bullish bravado'. (He's not Birmingham's best music writer for nothing.)

'Either Way', 'Drinking in LA' and 'Two Lovers' were greeted deliriously by the crowd, and by the time the joyous celebration of the end of a bad relationship, 'Took the Fun', got an airing, social distancing had become a distant memory. Me and my 'at-risk' wife decided to call it a night then, so I can't tell you if there was an encore.

I'm guessing I might have missed 'Cloudy Room' in the airy beer garden, but I left totally satisfied anyway, with all my lofty expectations met and then some. A great show.

The music press were once all over The Twang, hailing them as 'the best new band in Britain', but then doing them a huge disservice by labelling them forever as 'lad-rock', which was both wildly inaccurate and grossly unfair. By virtue of being real people with real lives, The Twang articulate the trials and tribulations of real people with real lives, be they cool dads or naughty lads, with an eloquence, wit and sensitivity unmatched in British music. And they do it to some banging tunes as well.

In this writer's opinion, and that of everyone who saw them at the British Oak the other night, The Twang are certainly NOT crap. I heard Phil Etheridge on a podcast the other day, sounding incredulous that 'we're some peoples' favourite band'. Don't sound so surprised, Phil, it's true. I'm one of them.

TOUGH COOKIE

Paul Cook is a mod, a Snobs legend, the founder of the Sunflower Lounge, a husband, a father and my mate. He was destined to be a DJ from a young age – his services were often in demand round our end when he was but 15 years old and already claiming a leadership role in the local mod squad. Darren Rigby was in charge of the European influence, I was the modernist philosopher, and Phil and Jim McLaughlin provided the muscle – vital when one considers the hostility of local skinheads and the fact that the rest of our firm wore eyeliner and couldn't knock the skin off a rice pudding.

Cookie was unchallenged as Head of Music, joined at the hipsters[1] to his portable cassette player, as we loitered without much intent on the streets of Birmingham. Whenever our parents went out, it was a case of Better Call Paul. 'Our mum and dad's goin' the Labour club tonight, you wanna come round and do a mod party?' There was a direct line to my big brother Dave at the pub in case any skinheads decided to gatecrash, and Cookie brought all the required records, which in truth was just The Jam's singles and albums, *Small Faces – Big Hits, 20 Mod Classics Volumes 1 & 2*, the *Quadrophenia* soundtrack, Booker T's *Green Onions* and the one I was most jealous of, 'Your Side of Heaven' by Back To Zero on 7in vinyl. It was at my house where he first learned to read a room.[2]

Always immaculately suited-and-desert-booted, his sartorial elegance and the impeccable taste his record collection suggests made him an Ace Face Mod and a lovely kid too. I think in all the years I've known him, we've only had one disagreement – when he said The Beatles were better than The Jam. Years later, I lightheartedly reminded him of this outrageous heresy and he denied saying it, so he couldn't have really meant it. So yeah, we always knew he was destined to be a DJ, we just didn't know he'd be such a great one.

1 By hipsters, I mean a type of trouser favoured by mods, not beardy blokes at Digbeth Dining Club.

2 Probably not true.

If my memory serves me correctly (and apologies if it doesn't), he first went behind the decks professionally for mod nights at the Outrigger/Ship Ashore, before starting his own legendary Sunflower night at Snobs, and then opening the Sunflower Lounge in Smallbrook Queensway. With no one else on the premises, he gave me the guided tour, proudly pointing out the images of our heroes Marriott and Weller adorning the walls of the downstairs room. Little did I know at the time, this room would eventually become the epicentre of the Birmingham independent music scene and be hailed as 'the best club in Britain for aspiring rock and roll stars' by none other than Noel Gallagher.

Paul went on to establish Temple Street Social and also put on some memorable nights at the Brown Lion in the Jewellery Quarter. One night, he booked the great Sam Rogers of White Flag Dares for a solo gig, with a sandwich board to that effect advertising the gig outside the pub. Now, there are at least two talented Sam Rogers in Brum, probably more, but on this particular occasion, the virtuoso saxophone-playing version walked past the Lion, saw the billboard and assumed he'd been booked to appear and had forgotten all about it. Luckily, he only lived round the corner and he hurried home to get his sax, only to find on his return that his namesake, the Britpop balladeer version, was ripping it up in the bar with an acoustic guitar and a set list of scorching covers and originals. The two Sams ended up playing together and putting on a thrilling collaborative show. Only in Birmingham!

More recently, Cookie had residencies at the Junction in Harborne, the Sun On The Hill in town and the Night Owl, a venue that was made for him and where I enjoyed seeing him the most. The UK's only bespoke Northern Soul club was one of his spiritual homes and years previously he had given Mazzy Snape – the Digbeth venue's driving force – her first gig. She didn't look back and she's still filling dance floors – well, she will be when we're allowed out.

It was at the Owl where, after I hadn't seen him for a few years, he told me all about his lovely wife Laura and the trials and eventual triumph that led to the birth of the couple's beautiful daughter, Amelie – it's no wonder she's so precious to them both. Unlike many men of his vintage, Paul was not shy about telling me exactly how much his family mean to him. He was by now an accomplished furniture restorer, occasional DJ, and a stay-at-home dad, supporting Laura's successful nursing career, and it was obvious from the omnipresence of his cheeky Steve Marriott smile that he was absolutely loving life.

Then, a few weeks ago, he contracted COVID-19, and an agonising vigil followed as his family and friends awaited daily updates via text messages from Laura, passed on to me by mutual friends Mark Eagles and the aforementioned Phil McLaughlin – thanks lads. It was a roller coaster ride of emotions and there were tearful phone calls between those of us who were rooting for him from afar, unable to visit and tell him how much we cared. For a while, through medication, unconsciousness and confusion, he was beyond the reach of human contact, so there was little chance he knew how desperately his mates were hoping, in my case praying to entities I was struggling to believe in, given what my mate was going through.

The wonderful staff at the QE never gave up on him, even when things appeared hopeless and, somewhat miraculously, prevented this evil illness taking away a wonderful, talented man from his beloved family and the many friends who love him almost as much. In normal times he would have had one-to-one care while so gravely ill, but during this crisis each nurse had responsibility for six of the poor stricken souls.

Every last one of those angels is a hero in the truest sense of the word. My niece Samantha is currently working seven days a week vaccinating people and I make no apology for taking this chance to publicly express my gratitude.

A rocky road still lies ahead for Paul and it will no doubt be a while before he's back doing what he does best – playing brilliant records and bringing joy to an audience. Bless you, Cookie; love lies waiting for you within your beloved family, the Sunny, the Owl and in the hearts of all your friends. It may be a long way off, but I can't wait to start annoying you again with requests.

Get well soon, old pal xx

Post script: Dave Scrivens, a friend of both Paul and I from the Birmingham mod scene, messaged me shortly after Paul's recovery. He was temporarily banned from Facebook (as usual) and was consequently out of the loop regarding our friend's illness. 'Why am I hearing about tributes to Cookie. He hasn't died has he?'

I brought him up to speed with the latest news and gleefully told him that although it had been a close call, Paul's life was no longer in danger.

'Thank God for that!' he replied. 'He's left me all his records in his will and I've got nowhere to put them.'

And that's that. Thanks for accompanying me on these beautiful, brilliant Birmingham nights.

SUPPORTING ACTS

George Francis
Adrian Goldberg
Robert Hayden
James Corden
Jerome Falconer
Kit Newey
Mark Lightwood
Martin Rissbrook
Neil Bates
Paul Caffrey
Paul Long
Russ James
A. A. Abbott
Lawrence Kempster
JulieAnne St Claire Jones
Martine Mccormick
Alistair Reed
Andrew Lapthorne
Prof Carl S Chinn
Carlos Malcolm
Chris Sutton
Cesar Perez Vega
Dean Williams
Debbie Bowen
Debbie Bowen
David Malys
Dominic Middleton
Victoria Perks
Jim McLaughlin
James Davis

Jason Donnelly
Jo Jeffries
John Gallagher
Jon Crofts
Jon Read
Karen Averby
Gavin Monaghan
Mark Hogan
Mark Purcell
Mazzy Snape
Megan Dickie
Michael Taylor
Nicholas Allen
Paul Cook
Peter Denny
Phil McLaughlin
Paul Cadman
Philip Young
Lee Piddington
Steve Cullen
Simon Griffiths
Simon Pitt
Chris Bushell
DJ Sainy
Tomasz Kulasik
Gerard James
Gareth Vernon Robinson
Wayne Benton
Graham Smith
Chris Waldron

SUPPORTING ACTS

Ben Groom
Brendan Phillips
Steve Byrne
Charlie Harkin
Clive Doyle
Clarry McDonald
Colin Hallum
Tracy Crawford
Daniel Wilkins
Daniel Sudbury
Rafal Sakwinski
Steven Gilfillian
David O'Mahoney
Dean Beresford
David Jackson
Mark Eagles
Earl Gilmartin
Gordon Bell
Steven Walker
Garry Turrell
Henry Plumridge
Amanda Hill
Andy Miller
Marklew Rice
Scott Roe
John James
Marcin Jankiewicz
Joanne Franklin
Josh Richards
Kate Mckenzie
Ian Kelly
Kevin Beecroft
Lee Cross
Liam Howard
Alex Lowe
Mark O'Shaughneeey
Lisa Bird
Mark Policarpo
Mark Moore

Michael Warnock
Michael Rose
Nick Knibb
Nicola May
Paschal O'Gorman
Paul Barnsley
Philip Shakespeare
Radoslaw Stochmal
Ryan Coyne
Richard Newcombe
Robert Hodge
Danny Malik Brown
Russell Joyce
Sam Davies
Sam Lambeth
Sam Pennell
Sarah Hempstock
Steve Wells
Sharon Walker
Dave Lynch
Sam Gamble
Sophie Evans
Kerri Pennell
Luke Drinkwater
Kurtis Cassin
Steve Hill
Tim Senna
Tony Whittaker
Dylan Toye
Tyla Challenger
Norman De langen
Warren Hanvey
Brad Edwards
Brad Edwards
Aaron Williams
Angela Jackson
Barrie Larvin
Christopher Leedham
Darren Kearney

Gary Lee

Jo Townsend

Jonny Amos

Kirk Whitehouse

Lee Byrnes

Matt Campbell

Matt Eagles

Nick Hennegan

Richard Franks

Richard Whitehead

Steve Watts

Sid Collins

Stacey Barnfield

Steve Berrington

Steve Hewitt

Richard Lacey

Liz Dexter

Tyler Cassin

Bod Phillips

Mickle O'Rourke